THE EARLY HISTORY OF THE TINNEVELLY CHURCH

HISTORY OF THE TINNEVELLY

THE RT. REV. BISHOP F. J. WESTERN

The Early History of the Tinnevelly Church

By the late Right Reverend F. J. Western

Author

The Rt. Rev. Bishop F. J. Western

PUBLISHED BY

TINNEVELLY CHRISTIAN HISTORICAL SOCIETY

Contents

Foreword

The Right Reverend F. J. Western was born on 24 February, 1880, in London. He was educated at Marlborough and Trinity College, Cambridge. At Cambridge he was senior Optime (i.e. second-class Honours) in the Mathematical Tripos in 1901. He then spent a year at Westcott House, Cambridge, a clergy training school, and afterwards took a teachers' training course at St. Mark's College, Chelsea, and obtained the Teachers' Diploma. In 1904 he joined the Cambridge Mission as a Lay Brother and came out to India soon after. He took up work in St Stephen's College, Delhi, as Professor of Philosophy. Mr. Sushil Kumar Rudra was then its Principal; he was the first Indian ever to be appointed Principal in any college in India. Nine Europeans worked under him. In 1909, Western became Head temporarily of the Stephen's High School, Delhi, succeeding the Reverend W. S. Kelly.

Within a short time Western joined an American Missionary, by name Stokes, who was working independently at Kotgarh, north of Simla. Together they formed the Brotherhood of the Imitation of Christ. The rule of the Brotherhood was a very severe renunciation of all creature comforts. The members of the Ashram had to live within Rs. 5/ - each per month. The aims were to show our Lord to the Indian people by service rather than by preaching, and to achieve a closer contact with them by living among them. Western lived like a Hindu Sadhu, and for some time took his abode among the Hindu boys in the Hindu students' hostel. The brotherhood went on for two years, when it suddenly collapsed as a result of Stokes's retirement. This was a great disappointment to Western. He returned to the Cambridge Mission and was made Acting Principal of St Stephen's College. He began again to lecture in Philosophy.

In 1914 he took charge of the financial department of the Mission, relieving Allnutt of part of his work. With great earnestness he now began to prepare for ordination. In 1916 he was ordained Deacon and in 1917, Priest. In 1917 Canon Allnutt died and Western succeeded him as Head of the Mission with the Reverend H. C. Carlyon as Head of the Brotherhood. His powers of organization and clear purpose made him invaluable as the first Rector of Delhi University. When Carlyon, too, died in 1919, Western became the Head of the Brotherhood as well as of the Mission.

During the 12 years that he was the head of the Mission, the Mission witnessed a period of steady growth and consolidation. For the first time Indians were admitted as ex officio Members of the Mission Council in 1918, and as Members of the St Stephen's Community in 1920.

He made great contributions to the Brotherhood, St Stephen's College, and to the University of Delhi. He was so useful because of his intellectual integrity, his devotion to duty, earnestness in learning the language of the people, his gift for constitution making, and above all, the simplicity of his deep piety.

From 1925 he was engaged in assisting Bishop Palmer of Bombay and Bishop Waller of Madras in drafting the Constitution of Canons and Rules of the Church of India, Burma and Ceylon. He proved himself an outstanding draftsman. Bishop Waller has often praised this proven capacity of Western and he says "after we all tinkered at some statement of profundity, Western would take it and cut its superfluities, and its meaning would then stand out clearl. The Constitution came into being in 1927.

When Bishop Tubbs was transferred in 1928 to Rangoon, Western was appointed Bishop of Tinnevelly.

It was a period of depression, especially in finance, when he took up the responsibilities of the head of the Diocese. The general depression was also due in part to the schism that had taken place in one part of the Diocese, Alvaner-Sevel area, when the Diocesanisation scheme was put into force during his predecessor's time. The Bishop's first endeavours were directed towards winning back those who separated themselves from the Diocese. The approach he made was one of love and kind actions. In the affair of the solemnization of the marriages among the Suthangamittes, for so they called themselves, the Bishop helped a great deal and enabled them to get state recognition for their marriages.

As the Bishop looked up he found "the field white with harvest. So he threw himself heart and soul into the evangelistic side of the Church's work. In one of his monthly letters to the Diocese he said that Evangelistic work was one of the important branches of the work in which the Pastorate Committee should take effective interest. It was a joy for him to conduct adult baptisms. His earnest desire was that there should be no family among the non-Christians of Tinnevelly who has not heard the Gospel. He longed to say, as Brotherton, that indefatigable missionary of the last century, said "there is no house in this District (Sawyer-puram-cum-Nazareth Missionary District) that has not heard the Gospel at its door-step". Western did not stop with a mere wish, or its expression. He induced the Pastorate and Circle Committees to organize regular preaching enterprises.

The Diocesan Evangelistic Band was reconstituted with the candidates for ordination in it during their periods of probation and placed under the supervision of a Superintendent,

More money was now necessary for the Evangelistic work. In order to meet the increased demands he tapped all the possible resources. One of such resources that received the Bishop's direct interest was the self-denial Offertory, which doubled and trebled during his episcopate.

He was not satisfied with mere baptisms; and so he took particular care to see that new Converts grew up in faith and developed in Christian character. He visited the new congregations as often as he could, and encouraged them to be of good cheer in the Lord and helped them grow in Christian knowledge.

The efforts of two learned ladies, the Misses Joy Solomon and M. M. Frost, for evangelising the barren North Tinnevelly blossomed in the Vidivelli Ashram at Sayamalai, founded by them in 1925. The Bishop was much interested in this project, and he took the two ladies himself to Sayamalai and blessed them. The work has grown wonderfully well, and the Ashram bears witness to what the Lord can accomplish through His devoted Servants, in so short a time as 25 years, when they surrender themselves and their all to Him for His work.

Another aspect of evangelistic service that a diocese has to do is foreign missionary work. Tinnevelly had already been blessed in this respect by its founding the Indian Missionary Society to work in the Telegu field... This idarling of Tinnevelly! was going through a period of financial strain in the Twenties. This fact attracted the Bishop's notice and he took it as a matter of his personal concern. As a man of prayer and faith, he took this to the Lord in prayer and began to work for it. Soon he saw the I.M.S. emerging out of its difficulties. The I.M.S. was also carrying on work among the hill tribes known as Palliars, on the Western Ghats between Tinnevelly and Travancore. To show his personal interest in the work, he went to see these people on the hills himself and it was a joy for him to confirm the Christian Palliars, those innocent souls in the faith of the Lord and of His Redemption.

Bishop Western was known to exert great efforts on the teaching Ministry and on the pastoral work of the Ministers. He chose able men, men of faith and devotion, for the ministry of the Church. He showed personal concern in the work of the clergy and in their private and Church life. No clergyman who went to the Bishop with his burden to unfold ever came out of his room with a disappointed and heavy heart. His wise counsels, loving advice and encouraging words cheered up the hearts of many a burdened man of God.

Churchworkers were regarded as much the Ministers of God as were the clergy, and the Bishop realised that they too should receive sufficient training for the work they did in the villages. To achieve this, he started Catechists-classes in the Theological Seminary. This class was a laudable move in the right direction, though unfortunately it was discontinued later, for reasons that a Bishop of Western's stature would never have .countenanced.

One source of troubles in the village congregation, the Bishop discovered, was to be found in the work of the itinerant preachers; false teachings also were spread by them. To save the Church from these evils, the Bishop instituted the practice of licensing such preachers, thus ensuring that only correct teaching was imparted by them. This practice closed the door against wrong instructions and heretical teachings.

The Bishop's keen interest in the welfare of the village Christians is seen in the fact that he made a close study of their day-to-day life. He discovered that there was much Hindu practice and beliefs still lingering among them, and in order to eradicate it, he realised, the clergy should have a first hand knowledge of this fact and he brought it to their notice. He instructed the clergy to do all that could be done to remove this evil.

Ignorance was another evil the Bishop had to combat. For this he encouraged the Night Schools and Adults' Schools in the Diocese, and rejoiced in their progress.

Bishop Western was one of those leaders with a vision. He saw clearly that the time when the leadership should, and would, pass into the hands of the Indian people was not far away. He steered the Diocese, therefore, towards it. One of the bold steps he took was to put an Indian in charge of the Diocesan Finance. The need for Indianisation of leadership was in the mind of the Bishop, even before he was consecrated. This is clearly seen in the constitution he helped to draft for the Church of India, Burma and Ceylon. In actual practice, responsibilities were gradually entrusted to Indians. Greater faith in their capacities was placed, and a greater share was handed over in the running of the Church, . including choosing our own Bishops.

The beautiful Chapel and the vast campus of the Theological College at Tirumaraiyur bear witness to the farsight of the Bishop.He saw in his vision a day when the Theological College would train not less than 36 students at a time and that for Tirunelveli alone. If that has not yet come to pass yet faith in the Christian enterprise and in the Master's lead demands that we believe the day is not far off when three or four times the number of clergy ordained now will be required for the Church in a few years to come.

Bishop Western was a scholar; Much can be said of his scholarship. In addition, he was an historian, as this wonderful book will vouchsafe. The amount of work he has put into this work and into another of its kind, the Register of Clergy 1778–1937, is staggering. These two volumes will, as the latter has already been, be the basis for future works on the history of this Diocese. He has also written the "Early History of the Cambridge Mission to Delhi" completed in 1951. .

The Bishop married Miss Grace New, a woman of great Christian accomplishments, who was the Secretary of the Mothers' Union in the Diocese, in the year 1934. During the short period she lived as the Bishop's wife, she proved herself a real "mother to the Christians of the Diocese of whom the Bishop was the "father". She won the hearts of all in her new capacity as she had in her old. She died suddenly in 1935, within a year after her marriage. This sad event clouded the latter days of the Bishop of Tenneyelly. Yet he carried on with the same vigour and faith, though many thought he would break down.

In 1938 Bishop Western retired and went back to his nativeer he became General Secretary of the Cambridge Mission to Delhi in London. He accepted membership in many communities of the S.P.G., the Indian Church Aid Society, and the Colonial and Continental Church Society. A life-long enthusiast for Church Union, he was a strong supporter of the Church Union in South India. So when he could not adhere to the policy of the S.P.G. with regard to the C.S.I. he resigned his membership of its committees.

He died on 24 November 1951, in England.

Bishop Western was a great administrator, scholar and philosopher. His devotion to the Saviour was outstanding. He was not only a Missionary, but also a Visionary for the Master. He was deeply interested in all those he worked with and served. He had a great fund of kindness which manifested itself again and again in unobtrusive but very practical ways. All these played their part in a life of outstanding service to His Master and the Church in India.

Preface

The Anglican Church in Tinnevelly, as it was untilen it has been part of the united Church of South India, a self-administering diocese, with a membership of 120,000, and a hundred Indian clergy, has a history of a hundred and seventy years. The earlier part of this period saw the development of the first mass movement towards Christianity among Protestant missions, and this had been preceded by the mass movement among the fisher Paravas of the coast which was initiated by St. Francis Xavier two hundred and forty years before, in 1542.

The present history has been written chiefly for the members of the Church in the Tinnevelly diocese. Until 1947, the diocese: included, as far as Anglicans were concerned, the adjacent districts of Madura and Ramnad, which now form a separate diocese of the Church of South India: hence this history includes the story of the early years of the Church in these districts also. It attempts to gather all that is known of the beginnings of that Church under the German nissionaries of the S.P.C.K., and to chronicle in considerable detail the early work of the C.M.S. and the S.P.G., so that the memory of pioneer workers, foreign and Indian, may be kept alive, and the fullest information possible may be made available of the beginnings of the congregations in the leading town and village centres of the diocese... In view both of the interest and importance in themselves of the Roman Catholic missions in Tinnevelly of the sixteenth to the eighteenth centuries, and of their influence on the later Protestant missions, a summary account of the former is prefixed to the main history of this book.

It is hoped, however, that this somewhat full description of early mass movements and of the first stages in the life of a Christian Church in South India, may also be of some interest to non-Indian students of missionary history and methods, even though the multiplicity of detail concerning longforgotten missionaries, and villages known to few outside Tinnevelly may in parts make somewhat difficult reading.For the benefit of such readers, an introductory chapter gives a slight sketch of the country and people of Tinnevelly.

Seventy years ago, Bishop Caldwell, who was one of the great leaders of the Tinnevelly Church in the later part of the nineteenth century - he worked in Tinnevelly as missionary of the S.P.G., and then as Bishop, from 1841 until his death in 1891 - gave a good deal of this history in his Records of the Early History of the Tinnevelly Mission. He had access to valuable unpublished material which is not now available, and any subsequent writer must owe much to his labours. He was not able, however, to use some important primary sources, and did not touch the history of the C.M.S. in Tinnevelly. In any case his book is out of print and not easy to obtain. The only existing general account of the work of the C.M.S. in the district is Mr Paul Appasamy!s small Centenary History of the C.M.S. in Iinnevelly. In the present history full use has been made of the early records of the S.P.C.K. missions in South India, and of the C.M.S., and some valuable unpublished material was found among documents preserved in the S.P.G. mission office at Tanjore. Further original material may still exist in Tinnevelly or elsewhere, but the present writer has not been able to trace it.

Tamil names of persons and places take many and sometimes strange foris when written in Roman characters by "German, French, or English writers of different periods; in nearly all cases these have here been reduced to a standard transliteration. The system of transliteration here adopted is a simplified one, no distinction being made between the identall and retroflexi tis and dis, the different nasals etc., it is hoped that the resulting forms will only in a few cases be ambiguous to those who know the Tamil language and the Tinnevelly district, while they will be understandable and pronounceable by foreigners. Well-known names such as Palamcottah (Palaiyankottai) or Tuticorin (Tuttikudi) have been given their usual English forms. Foreigners should note the following rules of pronunciation:

CONSONANTS may be given their usual English values. But

(i) Doubled consonants should be pronounced double, as in English hyphenated or separate words; e.g., tt as in "hot tar" and not as in "butter",

(ii) G, when not initial in a word or element of a Compound word, is used to represent a palatal sound similar to that of ch in the German sprechen.

(iii) gn stands for a letter the sound of which is roughly 'ny!

VOWELS a as English u in 'but'

a as English a in 'father'

e as English e in 'red'

e as English a in 'day'

i as English i in 'pin'

i as English ee in 'deem'

o as English o in 'of'

o as English o in 'blow'

u as English oo in 'good'

u as English oo in 'food'

ai as English ai in 'aisle'

The following are the meanings of certain common elements in piace-names:

-patti, -úr - Village

-nagar, -patnam,-puram - Town

-kottai - Fort --kudi - the abode of some particular caste, e.g., Idaiyan-kudi, Herdsmen's town.

-kulam -tank!, an artificial pond or lake.

-pettai - Market.

-vilai - Field,

The following religious worús frequently form part of Christian personal and place names:

Anbu - Love

Anugraham Arul - Grace

Asírvadam - Blessing

Deva - God

Gnanam - Spiritual wisdom

Kirubai - Grace

Pragasam - Brightness
Sagayam - Help
Samádanam - Peace
Sandosham - Joy
Sattiyam - Truth
Visuvasam - Faith

Acknowledgements

Published by:
TINNEVELLY CHRISTIAN HISTORICAL SOCIETY
04633-290401, +91 91767 80001,+91 75388 12218
https://christianhistoricalsociety.in
https://tchsportal.co.in/
Email : christianhistorical@gmail.com

The Early History of the Tinnevelly Church
in English
By Rt. Rev. Bishop F. J. Western

Prologue

Chrisitian Historical Society, a Christian researchers fellowship which empower, engage, enrich christian history and preserve Christian contributions to indian society. Christian Historical Society itself run by volunteers, theologians and Historians. Last three years our society has done various projects like field research, digitization, multimedia podcasting, social media proclamation for the goodness of Indian christianity and the Kingdom of God. Especially for the empowerment of future christian generations, our society publishes a Christian History research periodical called "Christhava Varalatru Suvadugal". For the Enrichment, and Engagement of christian knowledge Chrsitian Historical Society republishes the old christian books.

CHAPTER ONE

THE COUNTRY AND PEOPLE OF TINNEVELLY

Tinnevelly lies at the southern end of the Indian peninsula on the eastward side, separated from Travancore on the west by the range of mountains known as the Western Ghauts which runs down to Cape Comorin. Its greatest length is about a hundred and twenty miles from Cape Comorin to its boundary with the adjacent district of Madura; its width increases from nothing at Cape Comorin to about seventy-five miles at the Madura border.

The country siopes very gently from the feet of the mountains on the west to the sea on the east. The river Támbraparni runs tlirough the middle of the district, and for about a mile each side of the river is a belt oi rich alluvial soil, on which rice is grown. Iwo good harvests are reaped every year, and the vivid green of the young rice gives one of the brightest colours that India can show. Near the coast in . the southern part of Tinnevelly is a wide belt of pure sand, partly marine, but largely consisting of a peculiar red sand, piled in great dune's known as teris. Their origin is ascribed to the action of the fierce and continuous winds of the southwest monsoon, which sweep' up vast clouds of dust from the dry. surface of the red loam skirting the base of the hills and deposit their burden near the coast over the plains to the east... Under the action of water and manure the red sand quickly converts itself to a black mealy soil of great : richness." (1). But even without water or manure, the téri country is productive, for it abounds with the palmyra palm, the roots of which, to obtain their nutriment, stretch downwards through the sand for as much as forty feet. This part of the country, in fact, goes generally by the name of the palmyra forest. The remainder of the country, as also Madura, up to the time with which this history is concerned, was largely covered with woods and jungle. It is now essentially an open country, and generally cultivated, largely with cotton, though there are considerable barren and rocky areas. The mountain range is covered with forest, which still shelters a good number of tigers and wild beasts, which sometimes make forays into the nearer parts of the plains.

As might be inferred from its situation, eight to ten degrees north of the equator, but in no part far from the sea, and protected by the mountains from the main effects of the south-west monsoon, the climate is warm and equable; the temperature ranging between 75° and 95° Fahrenheit. The rainfall is light, and the air slightly moist, far less so than in Central and Southern Ceylon (the northern part of which lies eastwards across the sea from Tinneyelly) or on the west coast of India, but never reaching the extreme dryness of the interior of the Indian continent.

For the purposes of our main story, the history of Tinnevelly may be briefly summarized. Except for the last threequarters of the eighteenth century, when it was under the Muhammadan Nawab of the Carnatics Tinnevelly, with Magura, was under Hindu rulers until the coming oi the British raj. From B.C. 600 to A.D.1500 except for a short period in the 14th century, the Pandya and Chola dynasties held sway, with their . chief port and centre of the pearl trade at Korkai, known to the Greeks at the beginning of the Christian era as Kolkhoi; a. later chief port was Kayal, of whichi Marco Polo wrote in 1292:

"Cail is a great and noble city, and belongs to: Ashar, the eldest of the five brother-kings. It is at this city that all the ships touch that come from the west, as from Hormus, and from Kis; and from 'Aden, and all Arabia, laden with horses and with other things for sale... The king possesses vast treasures, and wears upon his person great store of rich' jewels'"

Marco Polo also gives a description of the pearl fishing on this coast.

In the sixteenth, seventeenth, and early eighteenth centuries, the Nayaka Hindu dynasty ruled from Madura, and under them a number of feudal chiefs known as Poligars ("holders of camps") By the middle of the 18th century, shortly after the rule, or at any rate the over-lordship of the Tinnevelly and Madura country had come into the hands of the Nawab of the Carnatic, there were thirty-two of these hereditary chieftains in Tinnevelly, and an equal or larger number of Madura, each of whom had entrenched himself in a fort and surrounded himself with a large body of armed retainers. As an English officer in charge of an expedition against one of them in 1783 reported:

"Adverse to industry, they suffer their own possessions to lie waste, while they invade each other, and plunder their industrious neighbours. Such is the dread of these ravagers, that every district in the province has been forced to purchase their forbearance by enormous contributions," (2)

The East India Company first rendered help to the Nawab to control these Poligars in 1751, and from a date shortly · after this regularly maintained a garrison of sepoys, or · sometimes of English troops, at Palamcotta. From 1751 up to 1801 there was a series of "Poligar wars" or expeditions, smaller or larger, against Poligars, in which British-led : troops took the major part; the last two serious Poligar wars . were in 1783 and 1799, both against the ff Kattaboma Nayakall, whose fort at Panjalankurichi in eastern Tinnevelly was particularly strong, and who of all the Tinnevelly chiefs was is the principal in power and in delinquency, excepting Sivagiri."

By the time of these last two Poligar wars, the .. administration of the Carnatic, including Tinnevelly and Madura, had been made over by the Nawáb to the Company, the Company paying to the Nawab one-sixth of the revenue: this arrangement lapsed in 1785, but in 1790 the Compariy by unilateral action Hassumed the management of the Nawabis countryll, and finally in 1801, the whole of the Carnatic was formally ceded to the Company, and the period of the British peace began.

'Of the many Hindu castes and sub-castes, three form together more than half of the total Hindu population of Tinnevelly, and need some mention here: Vellalas, Maravas, and Shanàrs, or, as they are now called, Nádars. The Vellalas are the great farmer caste of the Tamil country, and though Sudras in the strict Brahmanical reckoning, by common consent rank next to Brahmans in the social scale. The Maravas are of a somewhat similar standing: during the seventeenth and eighteenth centuries they were chiefly known as the followers of the Poligars, most of whom were themselves Maravas. "Bold, active, enterprising, cunning, and capricious, this class constituted themselves, or were constituted by the peaceful cultivators, their protectors in times of bloodshed and rapine when no central authority capable of keeping the peace existed... The feudal chief received a contribution from the area around his fort in consideration of protection afforded against armed invasion. His servants of the same caste, spreading themselves among the villages, received fees and sometimes rent-free land for undertaking to protect the property of the villagers against theft, or to restore an equivalent in value for anything so lost,it(4) At the present day they are cultivators like others, though somewhat more bold and lawless. Ramnad, the district lying eastward of Madura and running down to the point of Dhanushkodi and Adam's Bridge, which ever now almost completely joins Ceylon and India, was known as "The Marava Countryll, and the Maravas are said to have originally come from there and the country north of Ramnád. The Raja of Ramnád was formerly one of the greatest of the Poligars; he is now the. chief of a "zamindári" or estate under the Madras Government.

The Shanàrs, or Nádàrs, among whom the mass movements to Christianity took place at the beginning of the nineteenth century, as will hereafter be told in detail, are appreciably. lower in the Hindu social scale than either the Vellalas or the Maravas, and at best on the edge of the regular caste system. Their ancestral occupation was the cultivation and climbing of the palmyra palm, a tree of multifarious economic uses. The juice, to extract which the slender branchless stem must be climbed for sixty feet and more and then cuts made in the flower stalks from which the juice drips into pots, gives sugar, and when fermented, toddy; the fan-like leaves are used for roofing, mats, baskets, etc., and the tree itself when cut down gives pillars for houses and boards for general carpentry work..

It should be noted that during the last century, considerable proportions of the members of every caste have taken to other occupations than their hereditary ones. In particular, many of the Nádàrs have taken to trade, teaching, and other professions.

Below the accepted caste of Hinduism come the outcastes, whose not only touch but (until quite modern days) even sight pollutes the Brahmin or other high-caste many of these the Pallas and the Parayas (whence the English ipariah!!) may for our purposes particularly be mentioned.

A typical Tinnevelly village in the early days of British rule ilmust be conceived as formed of some seventy families of landholders', either Brahmins or Sudras, employing eighty-three families of serfs in agriculture, and about a hundred and forty other families, artisans, barbers, washermen, etc., to minister to their other wants and those of one another, There were one or more often fine temples dedicated to Siva or Vishnu for the landowners, and many little devil shrines and sacred trees for the benefit of the lower castes. The landowners had always the complete command of the village : servants, and could refuse the use of barbers, washermen, or watchmen to recusant members of any of the other classes." (5)

The town of Tinnevelly, on the Tåmbraparni, was the ancient capital of the district, while Palamcottá, only two miles from it, was a more modern one; Palamcottah, (as its name, literally "camp-fortif denotes) originally grew up as a fort to protect Tinnevelly, and it retained its character as an important fort until the end of the eighteenth century, Madura, with its immense temple which may be described as an epitome of the Hinduism of South India, on its grosser side, was the ancient capital and is now the chief town of the district named after it: other leading towns in the Tinnevelly district are Srivilliputhur in the north-west, Koilpatti on the road from Tinnevelly to Madura, Srivaigundam on the Támbraparni, and Tuticorin, the coast port.

NOTES AND REFERENCES - CHAPTER I

1) <u>Gazetteer of the Tinnevelly District, ed. 1917</u>

2) Colonel Fullarton, the commanding officer of an expedition against the Poligars in 1783: his report quoted by Caldwell, History of Tinnevelly, p.107.

3)Colonel Fullarton, ut supra, p.149. Kattaboma Nayakal was the title of the heads of the family of the Poligars of Panjalamkurichi. The one referred to by Col. Fullarton in the passage quoted was the second who is so entitled in the British records, the third was captured in the 1799 expedition, and was hung at Kayattár. The place of his execution is still marked by a large heap of stones by the le trunk road from Palämcottah to Madras, and is regarded as being spirit-haunted. The last Kattaboma. Nayaka was hung at Pánjalamkurichi in the final expedition of 1801.

4). Mr A.J. Stuart, in the Government Tinnevelly Manual.

5) Mr A.J. Stuart, op. cit.

CHAPTER TWO

THE ROMAN CATHOLIC MISSIONS IN TINNEVELLY, MADURA AND RÁMNAD

Christianity first began in Tinnevelly shortly before the middle of the sixteenth century, among the Paravas of the sea coast. These were (and are) a caste occupied in the fishing industry, including the marketing of dried fish in the interior of the country, and at the time of which we are writing making their special profit out of the pearl fishery. But for a number of years they had suffered from the depredations of the Muhammadans. of the west coast, and in 1534 an armed struggle developed, in which the Paravas were being worsted. On the advice of a European Malabari who was on the coast engaged in ized the horse trade, they appealed to the Portuguese authorities, who had by this time been established at Cochin, Goa and other points on the west coast for some twenty years, and offered to become Christians if the Portuguese would take them under their protection. . A deputation was sent to Cochin, their proposals were accepted, the members of the deputation were at once baptized, and an expedition was sent round to the east coast, which speedily dispersed the Muhammadans. Some Franciscan Fathers accompanied the expedition and baptized, it is said, twenty thousand of the Paravas, but left the coast again, and only paid a few short.visits in subsequent years. Some young Paravas were brought to Goa to be trained for the priesthood, · and some were sent on from there to Lisbon for the same purpose.

Eight years later, in May 1542, Francis Xavier, of the recently founded Company of Jesus, who had longed for, and when the opportunity came, eagerly accepted the work of a missionary to India, landed at Goa, where he at once began to work ardently in the hospitals and prisons, and in public catechisings for the Christians. After a few nonths, however, with the approval and perhaps on the initiative of the Vicar Episcopal, he decided that he must go to help the Parava Christians, and he sailed at the end of September in the ship of an officer who was going to Tuticorin to supervise the pearl fishery on behalf of the Portuguese government.

He landed at or near Cape Comorin, and made his way thence on foot up to Tuticorin, which he reached in two or three weeks. He knew, of course, nothing of the language, but had. with him three Indian priests, or perhaps students for the priesthood, from Goa as interpreters. He at once discovered that the Paraya Christians were such in nothing but the fact of their baptism.

"I at once tried to find out what they knew about our Lord. On the articles of the faith, I asked them what fresh beliefs they held after their baptism; I could get no other answer than We are Christians. They do not understand our language, and know nothing of the Christian law, or of what they should believe,

He therefore went on slowly from village to village for the sixty miles up to Tuticorin, preaching, baptizing children, and caring and praying for the sick.

!!I have baptized all the unbaptized children. Many of them were very young, that cannot discern between their right hand and their left handh. Those who were somewhat older left me no time to say my office or to sleep, I must teach them a prayer. I began to understand that tof such is the Kingdom of Heaven; 1 it would have been wicked to try to escape from such holy importunity, So I set myself to teach them to confess the Father and the Son and the Holy

Spirit (in the sign of the cross then the Creed, the Our Father, and the Hail Mary. I have found some of them very intelligent; if there were someone to teach them the Faith, I am sure that they would be good Christians,"

Arrived at Tuticorin, he stayed there for four months, getting translations made of the most necessary items in Christianl: instructionx(12)

X This should read(2) not (12)

They talk Malabar (Sc., Tamil); my language is Basque. So I got together the best taught among them, I sought out men who could understand both their language and ours, and we set to work. We have spent long days in preparing the set prayers; first the sign of the Cross with the profession of faith in One God in Three Persons, then the Creed and the Commandments, the Our Father, the Hail Mary, the Save us, Queen of Heaven, and the Confession."

He also translated an instruction hon what a Christian is, on heaven and hell, and on those who go to the one and to the other. These first translations were, naturally, crude and full of errors. St. Francis himself came to know of some of them, and tried to correct them; in 1544 he wrote to one of his colleagues:

"In the Creed, where it says enqubenum (sic, for enakku vendum, I need, or, I want) instead of venum, put vichuam (vi suvasam, faith, or belief). Venum means 'I wish for!, and vichuam means 'I believe'. One must say, 'I believe in God', not, I wish for God"

His translation was corrected a few years later by Fr. Henriquez (of whom later, but in the opinion of de Nobili it was still so barbarous as to be a real obstacle to the spread of Christianity among educated Hindus; it remained in use, however, on the Fishery Coast up to the end of the eighteenth century.

Having finished his translations and learnt them by heart, St Francis proceeded to put them into use.

"I went through the whole town, called together by a bell the children and such adults as I could, and taught them twice daily, two hours shortly after sunrise and two hours. at sunset, so that the prayers should be learned in the course of a month. I bade the children teach what they had. learnt to their parents, and all others in their home."

On Sundays he taught the whole congregation in detailed catechism style, making them repeat phrases after him. If there · were persons to be baptized,

" I make all, and especially those who are to be baptized, repeat the general confession, and then the Creed. At each clause of the Creed I ask them, iDo you firmly believe this?! Yes!. I repeat to them the commandments of Jesus Christ which they must keep in order to be saved, and then I baptize them. We finish all cur prayers with the "Save us, Queen of Heaven"

In addition to this work, his days were more than filled up wi th pastoral work; visiting the sick or praying and reading the Gospels over sick persons who were brought to him, baptizing infants, burying the dead, giving advice to individuals. He also had discussions with the Brahmans, but found among them few of any learning.

After four months, he left Tuticorin, and for nearly a year toured the villages of the Parava coast, that is, from Védalai near Rámnad, sixty miles northwards from Tuticorin, down to Cape Comorin, following in each place the same programme of teaching. Many were converted, and in some cases he baptized an entire. Village; he wrote that when he left there were thirty Christian congregations along the coast. He left catechists in the chief villages, and copies of the prayers in each Village, ordering that those who write could should make more copies, and that the people should repeat the prayers daily, and come together on Sundays to repeat them.

In December of 1543 he went to Goa to fetch helpers for the work, and returned in the following February with a lay brother of the Company, two priests, one Spanish and one Indian, and one, or perhaps two or three, laymen. While at Goa, he was able to arrange that the tribute paid by the pearl fishery to the Portuguese government should be allocated to the maintenance of catechists on the Fishery Coast.

He stayed on the Coast again until November 1544, and a number of his letters are extant written from various of the coast villages; about twelve from Manapped, where he made more than one stay of several weeks, and others from Alandalai, Virapandiyapatnam (adjacent to Trichendúr), Punnaikayal, and Tuticorin. He then passed on to south Travancore, where he made many converts among another lishing Caste, the fiMacuas, or Mukkuvas. His work then carried him to Cochin and Goa, and then on a missionary expedition of more than two years to the Moluccas, and he could not visit the Fishery Coast again until February 1548, and then only for about a month.

By this time, reinforcements of missionaries of the Company had reached India, and four of them were working on the Fishery Coast, including Fr. Antonio Criminale and Fr. Henri Henriquez. The work on the Coast was by now regularly organized into three districts, the Father in charge of each district having under him one or two Indian priests and some catechists. Teaching was given daily to the children, to girls in the morning and to boys in the evening, and weekly to the adults, to women on Saturdays and to men on Sundays.

St. Francis gathered the missionaries, with the four Indian priests who were working with them, for a sort of conferenceretreat of ten days at Manappad, and on his departure appointed Fr. Criminale as superior of the mission, and gave general instructions for the conduct of the work. Above all he urged that the missionary, while exercising firmness, and where needed, even severity, must seek to make himself loved. .s? Once morell, he ended his directions, ll make yourselves loved by kind words and kind actions.p?

St. Francis visited the coast once more for one or two weeks in September-October of the same year. By this time, Fr. Henriquez had so far advanced in his knowledge of Tamil às to have prepared a Tamil grammar and a dictionary.

At this point the direct connexion of St. Francis Xavier with. Tinnevelly ends. He was, however, appointed by St. Ignatius as

Provincial for India of the Company of Jesus, and acted as such for a short time in 1552, when he spent a few months at Goa and Cochin between his visit to Malacca and Japan in April 1549 to January 1552 and his final departure to Malacca, Singapore, and China. He died on the little island of Chang-chwen near Macao in December 1552, a young Chinese convert being his only companion, at the age of forty-six.

In the preceding pages we have given him the title of Saint, and thereby anticipated historically the official judgement of the Church, though not that of his contemporaries in India and particularly in Tinnevelly, who already regarded him as such. They had seen him in his days of incessant labour for the good of their bodies and souls, and in his nights of prayer; they had seen a self-denial which amazed them and a love to young and old which enthralled them; it is no wonder that they already believed that he had wrought miracles. Of later estimations of him, we will quote only one, that of the Dutch minister Philip Baldaeus, who, a hundred years later, unsuccessfully attempted to draw the Parava Christians over to Protestantism(3):

"He was a religious teacher of a holy and indescribable zeal such as is rarely to be found; and if his religion had been ours, he would certainly have been honoured by us as a second Paul. His zeal, his assiduity, his devoutness and other virtues should rightly in any case stir all pious persons not to be negligent in the Lord's work. Who among us does not know that if the yaliant deeds of the Jesuits had not arousec tlie. Franciscans from their dreamy slumbers and upheld the tottering throne of Rome, the Roman Church would long ago have fallen in ruins? My thought can hardly grasp the abilities and gifts of Xavier in furthering the cause of Christ; far less can my weak pen express them. When I consider, either his indefatigable labour in pouring drop by drop the holy dew of the Gospel into large and small vessels, or his immovable patience in adversities I can only say with Paul, "Who is sufficient for these things?i. . We can rightly wish that Xavier had belonged to us, "Since thou1 was such, would that thou wert or hadst been ours'.

During the four years that elapsed between the last visit of St. Francis to the Fishery Coast and his death, continued to develop, particularly under the charge of Fr. Henriquez, who became Superior of the mission when Fr. Criminale was killed at, védalai in June 1549 in a raid by the soldiers of the Madura Nayaka prince. Fr. Henriquez built a seminary at Punnaikayal, which passed on its best pupils to the Quilon seminary, hospitals both for Indians and for Portuguese, and chapels in several of the villages; the first regular church seems to have been that built at Tuticorin in 1582. He also appointed devout and educated converts as lay helpers, who would supervise the catechists, baptize infants, and help in other ways. · He is also to be remembered as the first missionary who gained some real knowledge of Tamil and set the standard of knowledge of the vernacular which was thereafter followed by the Jesuit missionaries.

Fr. Henriquez continued to be the Superior of the Fishery Coast mission until his death in 1600. By this time there were seventeen Fathers working the mission, of whom one was at Madura, and one assigned for work in the interior of Tinnevelly. The mission stations on the coast, were Tuticorin as the headquarters, Mannar Island; Vémbár, Punnaikayal, Virapandiyapatnam, Manappad, and Periyapatnam.

From 1600 onwards the history of the mission can be separated into three branches: the Madura Mission, which came to be the largest and the centre of the whole work of the Society in South India, the Coast Mission; and the work in the interior of Tinnevelly, which was partly connected with the former and partly with the latter....

In connexion with their trade in dried fish, Paravas resided at various towns and large villages in the interior, and in particular there was a group of them at Madura; and Madura: was opened as a mission station in 1595, under Fr. Gonzalve Fernandez, who before long built a church and a hospital, and opened a school in which a Brahman catechumen taught Hindu children. He had, however, no success in mission work among other castes than the Paravas.

Then in 1606 Fr. Robert de Nobili came to Madura, and soon afterwards started work among the higher castes on the new and daring lines for which his name has become farious. The higher caste Hindus, including in this term not only Brahmans but other castes much lower in the Hindu scale, but yet within caste, if only Sudras, such as the Vellalas were invincibly prejudiced against the Christianity which Crime to them through: the Portuguese and the out-caste converts. In the Portuguese pranguis (firangis, or foreigners) they saw it caste of men who were themselves eaters of beaf, and wearers of shoes in their churches, and who received personal services from the lowest castes, from which also practically all their converts had come. However much, therefore, the Christian teachings might be admired, to become a Christian meant to become a prangui or its equivalent a pariah, a thing as unthinkable for a caste Hindu as it would be for any civilized man to adopt a religion which entailed the eating of carrion. De Nobili therefore sought to break this conception of. Christianity by a far-reaching accommodation of missionary practice to the Hindu prejudices. He proclaimed himself to be, not a prangui, but a Roman (which he was) of the royal or warrior caste, 'adopted the dress and life of a high-caste sannyasi, allowed himself to be served only by Brahman servants, broke off all but the most secret connexion with Fr. Fernández and any other Portuguese or low-caste Christians, and built a separate church for himself in the Brahman quarter of the city.

On another side, de Nobili set himself the task of learning the doctrines of the higher Hinduism and of expressing Christian teaching in its tèrms, and succeeded to a remarkable degree in attaining at any rate the first of these aims. He acquired a complete mastery both of the higher Tamil and of Sanskrit, and was able to meet the most learned Brahmans on more than equal terms in religious debates. He published what he gave out to be a "Fourth Veda" containing the Gospel history and the doctrines of Christianity.

By 1611 he had baptized eighty-seven persons of good caste, and by 1623, three hundred. In 1638, with the approval of his ecclesiastical superiors, he developed a system for combining work among the low castes with that among the higher castes which was thenceforward followed in the mission; besides the brahman-sannyási missionaries, other missionaries joined the work as pandára-Swamis, dealing openly with the pariahs and other low castes, yet as Pandárams, or "religious? who had renounced the world, able to have connexion in religious matters with the brahman missionaries, though not able to live or eat with them.

De Nobili himself was in 1648 sent for his health's sake to Jaffna, and from there to Mylapore, where he lived in seclusion for some years, still maintaining habits of extreme asceticism, ana died in 1656. By this time there were abuut a thousand Christians connected with the brahman Fathers of Madura and Trichinopoly, and over two and a half thousand low caste Christians in the Madura, Tanjore, and Trichinopoly districts. It appears that only a few of the higher caste Christians were at any time actually Brahmans, the majority being of the Sudra castes, such as the Velialas.

For nearly a hundred years more the Madura Mission continued on these lines, and there was a large and steady extension of Christian congregations over a huge area, extending to Pondicherry in the north-east and to Mysore and Golconda (Hyderabad) in the north and north-west, as well as in the Marava country eastward of Madura and in Tinnevelly to the south. From 1703 the French Jesuits took over the work northwards and westwards from Pondicherry From time to time, in one district or another, both the Christian converts and the missionaries suffered severely from the effects of wars, which were invariably accompanied by wide-spread devastation and famine, and from direct and often savage persecution. Thus in the Marava country, there were severe persecutions between 1686 and 1695, and Fr. (later the Blessed) John de Britto was martyred at Woriur in 1693; there was then peace for some years, and the mission flourished, but there were persecutions again in 1710, 1714, and 1715. Various times of persecution are also reported in Tinnevelly, and indeed in every district in which the mission worked.

Particularly in the eighteenth century, the Madura Mission had to meet serious opposition to the principles and methods which had been developed by de Nobili and followed by his successors. A Bull of Gregory XV in 1623 sanctioned the wearing of the Brahman thread as merely a mark of social rank and office, and the regarding of Hindu rules of bathing as a matter of hygiene. But in 1704 the Cardinal de Tournon, who was sent out to India to deal with what had come to be called the question of the Malabar rites, gave directions which considerably restricted the amount of the accommodation to Hinduism which the missionaries might practice, and in particular ordered that the sacraments must be given to sick pariahs even if it entailed the brahman missionary entering their houses. These directions were endorsed by the Holy See in 1706, though with a clause which indicated the possibility of further consideration of the matter. The Fathers of the Madura Mission evaded putting the directions into practice, and they and their friends continued to urge their case for thirty-three years more; but the directions were confirmed by Rome in 1727 and again in 1734, and an order was given in 1739 that all bishops and missionaries should take an oath of obedience to them. Finally in 1744 a Bull of Benedict XIV confirmed the previous decisions, and at the same time, however, permission was given that some of the missionaries should work exclusively among the low castes.

These decisions led at once to the building of entirely separate churches for the low and for the higher castes; previously (since 1650) the plan had been followed of building double churches, of two entirely separate parts and with separate entrances, but arranged so that the low-caste Christians could see the high altar in the higher-caste part of the church through a doorway. Separate low-caste churches were thus built shortly after 1744 at Madura, at Kámaiyánayakanpatti (then one of the chief stations in Tinnevelly), and at Tinnevelly.

A few years later, the enforcement of the papal decrees and the establishment of the low-caste missionaries had the eifects which the Fathers of the mission had anticipated; the Sudra Christians out-casted all of their number who had any connexion with the low-caste missionaries, and there was a large number of apostacies, which different authorities estimate at from ten to fifty thousand. The total number of Christians in connexion with the mission at that time is given as 120,000 in the Marava country and on the Fishery Coast, 150,000 in. Madura and Trichinopoly (Madura here probably including the interior of Tinnevelly), 80,000 in the Carnatic, and 35,000 in Mysore.

The Fathers of the Mission certainly felt the decrees as a severe blow to their work, but there soon followed the real catastrophe of the practically complete collapse of the mission when the Portuguese government deliberately set itself to destroy the Society of Jesus and succeeded in doing so. In 1759 all the missionaries on the West Coast were deported, and the supply of funds to those in the interior and on the East Coast was cut off; and the Societywas formally suppressed by Clement XIV in 1773. Some of the missionaries in the interior and on the East Coast remained until they one by one died off, and some Goanese priests were sent from the West Coast, but it is hardly too much to say that the work throughout the area of the mission was abandoned for more than sixty years. At a later point in this chapter we shall briefly describe the history of this dark period of the Roman Catholic missions in South India, but we now turn back to follow the history of the Parava mission from 1600 onwards, and the growth of congregations in the interior of the Tinnevelly district.

Between 1600 and 1773, the Parava mission had its own fluctuations of prosperity and hardship. From 1609 to 1621 the Jesuit Fathers had to withdraw from the coast on account of dissensions with the Bishop of Cochin, and there was a serious collapse of the congregations, which was enhanced by a twelve years failure of the pearl fishery. By 1616, as a Father reported, most of the churches had been destroyed, many of the Christian villages were almost deserted and thousands of the Christians scattered among the heathen had reverted to Hindu practices; only six thousand Christians remained where there had been more than twenty thousand.

The Fathers were able to return in 1521, and the work again made progress; in 1644 the total number of Christians under the twelve Fathers working on the coast was about twenty-six thousand, including some fifteen hundred in the interior of Tinnevelly.

In 1658, the Dutch took Tuticorin and the Fishery Coast, expelled the Fathers from the coast towns, and endeavoured to convert the Parayas to Protestantism. We have the account of their first chaplain, Philip Baldaeus (4):

"The Paruas ever since this union with the Romishi Church, are such zealots in that religion, that there are scarce any hopes of ever bringing them over to our side; their ignorance in religious concerns being such, that besides the use of their beads, and making the sign of the cross, they know nothing of the true fundamentals of the Christian religion they pretend to profess. In the year 1661, I was ordered to take a journey from Tutecoryn to Coulang (Quilon), to visit the churches along the sea-shore, and endeavour to introduce a reformation there; but my endeavours proved ineffectual by by reason of the great number of popish priests yet remaining in that country.!!

In a later passage he says that the Parava Christians were able to say by heart the Creed, the Our Father, the Ten Commandments, and the Hail Mary; and that after his departure, "the reverend Mr John Fereira Almeyua, a native of Lisbon, was for a whole year employid in the reformation of the Paruas, but with less success than myself",

owing to his being a renegade from Roman Catholicism. Baldaeus remarks of Tuticorin that it

"is properly no more than a large village, without walls, ditches, or gates; it has three spacious churches, and abundance of goodly houses built of stone, which afford a good prospect at sea."

A little later, when the Dutch tried to force the Parayas to attend their services, the chief of the caste forbade any to go to the Dutch church, and only one man did so, whereupon the chief sent armed men, who killed him as he came out of the church, and the Dutch could do nothing. Subsequent Dutch governors, however, allowed the Fathers to return to Tuticorin, and by 1700 there were good relations between them and the Dutch authorities. It may be noted here that, the Dutch church in Tuticorin, the use of which finally passed to the Church of India, was built in 1750.

The main Christian villages on the coast in 1700 were from the south upwards, Periyatálai, Manappád,. Álandalai, Punnaikayal,and Tuticorin.

In 1719 there was a sort of rebellion of the Paravas against the missionaries, and Fr. Bertholdi was sent from Trichinopoly to assist in the restoration of order in the Church and in the renewal of spiritual life. He wrote in 1720 that

"Drawn into intrigues by their natural taste, and seduced by the Dutch, who made use of their passions to ruin secretly the Catholicism against which their open attacks had been unavailing, the Paravas had rebelled against their missionaries and driven them all from the coast by means of plots and of violence."

When he arrived, the storm had passed, arid the missionaries had returned, but there were still grave scandals within the Church. He conducted a month's Ignatian retreat at Tuticorin, which reconverted many, including Stephen da Cruz, the chief of the caste, and other, equally successful retreats at Punnaikayal and at Manappád.

In 1760 there were eight mission stations on the coast with a total of thirty-five churches.

We now turn to the development of Christianity in the interior of the Tinnevelly district. By 1600 Christianity was beginning to spread from the coast inwards, primarily among Paravas, but also among other low castes, and in 1600 one of the Coast Fathers was assigned to the work in the interior, The Annual Letter from the Mission to Europe of 1602 states:

"The Fathers have penetrated a little further into the interior, where they have five churches, and 2,400 Christians. At a place twelve leagues inland there is a church dedicated to St. Bartholomew, a little way outside a large city which was in former times the residence of the Náyakas and lords of the country. They hope with God's help to build up a large Christian community, for there are already about fifty Christians there, and they are negotiating with the lord of the country to build a church in the town itself; only the fewness of the Fathers has delayed things."

This large city must have been Palamcottah or Tinnevelly. (5)

In the next year it was reported that a Father had penetrated fourteen leagues into the interior, and had built nine churches. In 1621, after the twelve years absence of the Fathers from the Coast, of which we have previously written, the work in the interior was renewed. A Father made a long tour inland to visit and renew the congregations, and found about seven hundred Christians at Tirukalúr (near Srívaigundam), and Christians also at palayam, "the second most important town in the kingdom of the Nayaka', i.e. Palamcottah, or perhaps Tinnevelly.

By 1544, Tirukalúr had become a regular mission station, with a church and five hundred Christians. It was the only place in the interior which had a regular church, others having only small chapels. A list is given of the village congregations which the Tirukalúr Father visited; Srivaigundam (133 Christians), Pålayam (70), and Kayattár (18), a line of small congregations stretching to the north-west from Palamcottah through Víravanallúr up to Kadaiyanallúr, and also a few to the southwest near the hills, including Kalakåd.

From about 1050, tlie interior of time Iinneveliy district seems to have been worked from Madura, or even Trichinopoly, at any rate as far as the non-Parava congregations were concerned. Kayattár became a definite mission station in about 1680, but Kámaiyánayakanpatti superseded it as the missionary's residence in 1688.

In about 1680 the first Shanar congregation began with the conversion of a Shánar woman named Sandai at Vadaliankulam; a church was built there in 1685, and by 1701 it was made a mission station, and it and Kámaiyánayakanpatti were occupied up to the time of the break-up of the mission. In 1713 there were 4128, Christians in the Vadakankulam parish, who were nearly all Shanars. Some Vellalas were, however, converted there in about 1740. For some time during the eighteenth century, Gurukalpatti, a small village near Alankulam on the road from Palamcottah to Tenkási, was the place of residence of the missionary instead of Kámaiyánayakanpatti. The celebrated missionary and scholar Fr. Constant Beschi. resided there between 1713 and 1716, and it is said that on one occasion he was about to be killed by the Brahmans of the village, but was rescued by the Christians of Kayattar. Shortly after this event he was transferred to the Trichinopoly district, and worked there until 1740. In that year, on the Mahratta. invasion, all the missionaries had to flee from the districts occupied by the Mahrattas, and Beschi came down to Manappad and lived there from 1742 until his death iri 1746. (6)

We have already mentioned the Marava country, the southern part of which is now the Rámnád District, in connexion with the Madura Mission. A few more details may be added here. Mission work seems to have begun in the district in about 1660. In 1715 there were churches at several places on the coast, and the islands east and south-east of Rámnád. No churches are mentioned as being in the interior, but it is clear that there were a good many congregations, though with frequent disturbances and persecutions their number and strength continually varied. Fr. Rossi, who was working in the Marava kingdom in 1742, reported that in that year the Protestants of Tranquebar penetrated into the Marava country and he accused them of attempting, without any success. to seduce the Roman Catholic Christians, and to make converts among the heathen, by means of bribery and intrigues. The Protestant version of this will be found in our next chapter. Earlier, in 1731, Beschi had written from the Trichinopoly district that:

"A pressing danger threatens this mission from the Lutherans, who are animated with a hellish rage, and prowl around the fold seeking for prey!; three year's earlier he had found it necessary to write several controversial works against Protestantism.

As we have already stated, the Jesuit Fathers were expelled from the West Coast. in 1759, and the Society itself was dissolved in 1773.. A certain number of the Fathers on the.. East Coast and in the interior, however, remained, subsisting on the contributions of the local Christians, and continued to work under the Portuguese Archbishop of Cranganore and Bishop Of Cochin. In 1775 there were six Fathers remaining on the Tishery Coast, one in the interior of Tinnevelly at Vadakankulam, and one in the Marava country.

The Portuguese bishops did what they could for the missions by sending Indian or Indo-Portuguese priests from Goa, and as the Jesuit Fathers gradually died off, the work became entirely left to these priests, Oli the Coast there were Jesuit Fathers at Virapandiyapatnam, Alandalai, Manappád, and Uvari up to about 1790, Manappad being the last station on the coast that was occupied by a Father.

The French Société des Missions Étrangères, already established in Bengal and at Pondicherry, was in 1771 given charge by Rome of the Carnatic Mission of the Jesuits, and in 1776, 1778, and 1785 was given somewhat vaguely worded commissions to take charge of the Madura and Fishery Coast Missions. The Portuguese ecclesiastical authorities on the West Coast, however, still continued to have their jurisdiction over those districts, and when they did not actually oppose the work of the French missionaries, only offered a luke-warm cooperation with them, and did nothing to check the direct opposition which was offered everywhere by the Goanese priests. The French missionary society, therefore, thus hampered in its efforts and itself somewhat short of workers, was able to do practically nothing to help the Madura and Fishery Coast. Districts. At last the appeals of the French society's bishops for more definite powers were answered in 1836 by the formation of the Vicariates Apostolic of the Coromandel Coast and of the Madura Mission district, all the mission work of these areas being thus removed from the jurisdiction of the Portuguese bi shops. At the same time, at the request of the French Society, the Madura and Fishery Coast missions were again entrusted to the Society of Jesus, which had been re-established in 1814. The first Fathers of the new mission arrived in 1837. (7)

Up to the time of the deportation of the Jesuit Fathers from the West Coast, the Goanese priests had been trained by them; thereafter, according to the testimony both of the inissionaries of the French society and Ci the later Jesuits, the quality of these priests rapidly fell off. Most of them were Indo-Portuguese, and one authority says that they had all the defects and vices of the Portuguese and none of their good qualities. They had little knowledge of Tamil, were full of a sense of their own social superiority, were often drinkers and quarrellers, and knew no theology beyond the special privileges granted by former Popes to the kings of Portugal. A French missionary of the period describes them as being generally ignorant, lazy, and small-minded, and often setting the congregations against them by théir tactlessness. (8)

These descriptions of the Goanese priests may be slightly coloured by anti-Portuguese prejudice, but the Protestant missionaries at Palamcottah between 1820 and 1830 agree that most of them were ignorant and inefficient. There were, however, exceptions; Hough, writing in 1820, says that some were very well educated, and Rhenius in 1829 says of Mr. Piedade, the late Roman Catholic Vicar!, wyho had just left the district, that he has behaved very well during his stay here and appears to have faith and to value the Gospel."(9)

In any case, the Goanese priests were insufficient in number, and in general could not have fixed pastoral charges, but toured round to administer the Sacraments, nor do they seem to have received any supervision or help from their ecclesiastical superiors. Under these conditions, it was inevitable that the congregations should suffer serious losses in numbers, and far more serious losses in quality. Considerable numbers drifted back to Hinduism; some, we shall see in later chapters, found that Protestantism could give them the living beliefs and the help in the practice of the Christian life which the Roman Catholic Church was failing to give them; many remained Catholics in name, but with a disorganized and - demoralized Catholicism which became nothing but a matter of caste or group habit of certain outward observances.

The actual loss in numbers was probably not great among the coast congregations, and all the main congregations in the interior of Tinnevelly remained in being, though considerably reduced in numbers. Thus Hough reported in 1820 that. there were said to be some 30,000 Roman Catholics in the district of Tinnevelly (these presumably including those of the Fishery Coast); there were fifty-three churches, in connexion with each of which there was a catechist, and eight priests were working in the . district; there was one school, at Vadakankulam. Rhenius in 1823 mentions the churches at Tuticorin, Kombádi, Kayalpatnan on the coast, and Palamcottah, Tinnevelly, Péttai, Sivalaperi, Tirukalúr, Kayattár, Viravanallur, Tenkási, Vadakankulam, and Kalakkád in the interior. Many of the Roman Catholics, he says, were of respectable status, such as landholders and merchants. (10) From other sources we hear of surviving congregations in the Rannad district, including a small congregation at Rámnad, for whom Col. Martinez built a church in about 1803.

No great number turned to Protestantism. As we shall see in later chapters, some. Vellala Roman Catholics who came over were leaders of value in the first days of the congregation at Palamcottah in 1780 onwards, and the two first small village congregations of the Tanjore mission in Tinnevelly came from Roman Catholicism. In later years also there was a steady but not large stream of converts from Roman Catholicisin, both among the Vellálas and the low castes. But the Roman Catholic Shánar congregations contributed practically nothing either to the first Protestant mass movement among the Shánars in 1797 to 1203, or to the l'evival of that movement under Rhenius in 1827 and the following years. (11) Except for a small body of Parayas who came over in 1789-90, but who practically all went back to Roman Catholicism within a year or two, no Paravas turned to Protestantism.

The Jesuit Fathers who returned to Tinnevelly in 1837, therefore, found large congregations on the coast, and at least considerable congregations in the interior. At Palamcottah They found fifty Christian families, nearly all Parayas. But they could only report in the most gloomy terms upon the religious state of these congregations. Catechisms and public instructions and the use of the sacraments were unknown among them. On the coast

"Many old men could not even make the sign of the cross. Drunkenness had spread through all ranks and classes, even to women. The sanctity of marriage was forgotten; concubinage seemed to have lost its shamefulness. Surdays were kept like ordinary days. In many places superstitious practices and . sorcery were common. The revenues of the churches, their treasures, even their ornaments and sacred vessels had become the pi'ey of intriguing and greedy persons." (12)

The Fathers set to work to reconvert and build up the Church, but had only just begun this task by the end of the period covered by the present history, and we therefore end at this point our brief account of the Roman Catholic missions in Tinnevelly.

NOTES AND REFERENCES - CHAPTER II

(1) The information given in this chapter has been mainly taken from Fr. J. Bertrandis La Mission du Maduré (Paris, 1847-1854), and Fr. L. Bessels La Mission du Maduré: Historique de ses Pangous', (Trichinopoly, 1914); it has not seemed necessary to vive particular references. The account of St. Francis Xavier's work has been based on Fr. A. Brou's Saint Francois Xavier (Paris, 1922), which is said by Fr. Besse to give the best account of his work on the Fishery Coast.

2) Fr. Besse holds that St. Francis stayed at Manappad while preparing his translations. There is no direct evidence on the point, for St. Francisi account, written from. Goa in January 1544, gives no names of -places. After describing the process of translation of the prayers and the teaching of them, he says: If I stayed four

months in a large town of Christians,translating our prayers into their language and then teaching them; then, after speaking of the number of people who filled up his time, he goes on - I left a person in that town to carry on what I ad begun, and went on to other towns, doing the same in them"

It seems more natural to take it, as Fr. Brou does, that having arrived at Tuticorin after his first journey up the coast, he stayed there for his translation work.

3) Baldanus, Wahrhaftige ausführliche Beschreibung...

(Amsterdam 1672), Chap. 22, p.150. The English translation referred to in note 4) below only summarizes the passage here quoted.

4) Baldaeus, op. cit., in Lintot and Osborn's translation,

Chap. 22, pp. 5&4 ff.

5) Fr. Besse (op. cit., p.404) says in a footnote to the quotation:

"The name of this town is not given. In a report published in 1644 we find a church dedicated to St. Bartholomew at Manacadu, with sixty Christians. Manacadu, I am told, is an unimportant village near Srivai gundam."

But twelve leagues, which could not be less than 28-30 miles, and might be distinctly more, would bring one from the coast. far beyond Srivaigundam, and in fact to Palamcottah. The Manakkad would naturally be that which lies four to five miles north east from Palamcottah, near Sivalaperi. The Pleaguei. Appears to represent an hour's walking, and therefore anything between 2 1/2 and 3 1/2 miles.

6. For a nodern biography of Fr. Beschi. See F Father Beschi of the Society of Jesus (Trichinopoly, 1918).. Bp. Caldwell in his History of Tinnevelly (pp.238 ff.) gives an account of his life, and says

"He is said to have been buried in the chancel of the church at Manappad, but the oldest of the churches is now completely buried in the sand."

7. It must be explained that the difficulties between the French Société des Mission Étrangères and the Portuguese bishops of the

West Coast formed merely one chapter in a long controversy. In 1493, Pope Alexander VI had granted to Portugal the right of ecclesiastical patronage to be exercised over all countries conquered or to be conquered or discovered by Portugal, a monopoly of missions being thus added to a monopoly of conquest and trade, From the time, however, when an anti-clerical Government of Portugal extorted from Clement VI the suppression of the Jesuits, Portugal entirely failed to fulfil its side of the implied bargain by founding and endowing episcopal sees, seminaries and parishes and generally promoting the work of the Church. Hence at long last Gregory XVI: took action in 1836 by appointing Vicars Apostolic who depended iminediately upon the Holy See, and by abolishing the Goanese jurisdiction in the areas placed under those Vicarsi This action, however, being only unilateral, did not entirely close the question, for the Goanese priests and their superiors felt themselves bound by the authority of the King of Portugal. When the Jesuit Fathers began to take over the work on the Fishery Coast and in Tinnevelly, therefore, some of the Goanese priests refused to submit to this new authority, and a certain amount of confusion and trouble continued until a concordat was made between the Holy See and Portugal in 1860.

For the history of the Société des Missions Étrangères, see (Paris, 1. 'Abbé Adrien Launay, Histoire des Missions de l'Inde 1898).

8) Mgr. Laouenan, Archbishop of Pondicherry, quoted by Launay, op. cit., p. CXXVi; and M. Tesson, quoted by Fr. J. Bertrand, I,ettres edifiantes et curieuses de la nouvelle mission du Madure (Paris, 1865), p. 21.

9) Rev. James Hough, in A Reply to the Letters of the Abbé Dubois (London, 1824), p.105, and in a letter to the C.M.S. of 1820, for which see the C.M.S. MS. records, South India' series of volumes, Vol.I, pp. 261 ff; and Rhenius' Journal of Dec. 3rd, 1829 in the same series, Vol. VII, p.270.

10) Hough, 'loc. cit; Rhenius, in a paper drawn up for the C.M.S. giving a general dscription of the Tinnevélly district, in C.M.S. MS.

records 'South Indiai ut supra, Vol.III, pp. 183 ff.

11) It is to be regretted that Abbé Launay seems to accept as accurate the following remarks by Archbishop Laouenan, which can, with all respect, be only described as ludicrous:

"In Tinnevelly there was a flourishing Church chiefly composed of shanars of about 30,0CO souls. After the departure of their fathers, these poor people, finding themselves suddenly deprived of pastors, listened to the voice of a Protestant minister, the famous Schwartz, who presented himself to them in Jesuit dress and claiming to be the successor of St. Francis Xavier and Fr. de Nobili. Such were the beginnings of these flourishing Protestant congregations of Madura wiich now have 150.000 members"

12) Fr. A. Martin, one of the four first returned Jesuit Fathers, quoted by Fr. J.C. Houpert, Á South India Mission (Trichinopoly, 1937), p.68.

CHAPTER THREE

THE BEGINNINGS OF THE PROTESTANT MISSIONS IN RÁMNAD AND TINNEVELLY 1730 to 1790

Apart from a few individuals who may bave been instructed and baptized by Dutch chaplains at Tuticorin or some other trading post along the Fishery Coast, non-Roman Christians are not found in Tinnevelly until about 1770, and the first congregation grew up in about 1780. Fifty years earlier than this, however, there were one, or, two congregations of Protestant Christians in the Rámnád district, and these last, therefore, were the first representatives of:. the present dioceses of Tinnevelly and of Madura and Rámnád.

In 1706, Ziegenbalg and Plutscho, the first Protestant 11ssionaries to India, landed at Tranquebar as the first members of the mission established by King Frederick IV of t. Denmark, Tranquebar being then a Danish possession, ceded by the Rajah of Tanjore in 1621. For more than twenty years they "Vorked only in Iranquebar itself and the immediate neighbourhood; but in 1727 they found themselves able to extend their work into the kingdom of Tanjore, and congregations began to grow up at Tanjore itself and at Mahadevapatnam, about forty miles, southwest of Tranquebar. In 1729 somo families from near Rámnad in the Marava country, as it was then always called, came to Mahádévapatnam. They were apparently already acquented with the catechist there, Sattiyanádan, and were converted through him, and baptized at Tranquebar. They returned to their home, and from this time onwards there were some small groups of Christians in and near Rámnád, who formed an outlying branch of the Tranquebar mission.(1)

In 1730, through one of these Christians, the Tranquebar Mission was brought to the notice of the Rajah of Ramnad and . his court; the episode is worth recounting, although it led to nothing. The Christian, Savarimuttu, who was a soldier in the Rajah's service, told his friends and acquaintances about the Tranquebar missionaries and their charitableness, and presented to one of the court servants a New Testament which the missionaries had given to him. The story, and the New Testament, came to the Rajah, who caused a letter to be sent to the missionaries by the hand of Savarimuttu, the contents of which they give as follows:

N.N., a servant of the Raghunatha Tévar (the full title of the Rajah was Muttu Vijaya Raghunatha Sédupati Kátta Tévar) send us his greetings; they had been told by Madiya puli (Savarimuttu's Hindu name) that we had established many works of charity at Tranquebar; they had read the book which had been sent to them, and found that it contained noble teaching and many good things, and that the priests were teachers of the one most high God and laboured that all people should like themselves endeavour after godliness; we and our people would be well received if we would come to them, and if we wished to open good institutions there, the Raja offered to give us a village with the land belonging to it; if we had any foreign curiosities we might send them by the man who brought this; their friendship with us would last as long as the sun and the moon endured.

The missionaries built no great hopes on the polite phrases of the letter, but felt that they should not miss a possible opportunity, and sent a catechist, Diogo, with Savarimuttu, beai ing an answer in which:

We returned thanks for the letter to us and its gracious offers, and added the text? There is one God, and one Mediator, etc.,, expressing the vish that the name oi Jesus, as the Redeemer of the world and the Lord of blessedness, and the salvation earned by Him, might become known to all the people of the country from the highest to the lowest.

Diogo and Savarimuttu made a speedy journey, taking only nine days for the distance of about one hundred and forty miles, the way leading partly through forests, and near the sea-coast crossing many streams the depth and breadth of which varied with the state of the tide. Through Savarimuttu, Diogo, was granted an audience on the evening of his arrival at Rámnác, and presented the missionaries' letter. The Rajah having read the letter asked what a mediator was; the catechist answered, and presented to the Rajah a copy of the Iranquebar booklet.on The Plan of Salvation. There was some further conversation, and the Rajah repeated his offer of a village, in which the missionaries might build both a house for themselves and any institution, they might wish to set up.

At his inn, Diogo met the Rajah's umbrella-bearer, who told him to the wajah Han not been Bart; ized 2.5 a Foman Catholic, as 50m€ PEOPI.S Ve out, but haü ilearü some thing or Chiristianity. He was, however, devoted to polygamy, and kept fifteen eunuchs to attend on his wives, and these eunuchs had great influence in the court. Some time before, a Roman missionary had come to Rámnád, and the Fiajah had given him a yellow robe of honour and the village of Sarugani to settle in, and another Roman missionary had obtained leave to build a church in a village near Rajasingamangalam.

After a week, during which he visited several of the Rajah's ministers, Diogo obtained leave to depar visiting the Dutch settlement at Kilakarai, went to Valasai, some eleven miles north-west of hámnád, where most of the Christians were living, and held Sunday services for them. They were weak, il both in their knowledge and in their confession by word and by lifell, but desiring to learn. Their number seems to have been about twenty or twenty-five.

During the next six years the Rámnad Christians were only visited twice by catechists; and on the second occasion, in 1736, the catechists reported that they were becoming discouraged owing to the lack of attention which the missionaries had given to them and that in their strong desire to be admitted to Holy Communion they had almost resolved t.) join the Roman Catholic Church. They were; however, ready to wait for a promised visit by the native minister in the next year. This visit was duly paid by Aaron(2) in May 1737, when he stayed seven days at Valasai, and on his return to Tranquebar the Vellála catechist Joshua was sent to reside at Ramnád, with instructions to come to Tranquebar and report once a quarter.

Joshua met with great hostility from the Roman Catholics, who in 1738 beat him and pulled down his house; and after less than two years the missionaries thought it best to remove him, and neither he nor any other catechist thereafter resided in the district for more than a month or two. Both the pastoral care of the small groups of Christians in the Ramnad area and their own stability and growth were greatly hindered from 1730 onwards, not only by the hostility of the Roman Catholics, but still more by the disturbances caused by war. There were in fact few years between 1740 and 1772 in which Rámnád was free from war, either with some other local chief, or as involved in some way in the larger wars which · raged during these years in South India.

The Tranquebar missionaries, however, did their best for these distant and small groups of Christians by sending a Catechist or a native minister to visit then generally once if not twice a year. On Aaron's visit to them in 1740, he prepared some people for baptism and for the first time actually baptized them in the district itself. He also celebrated the Lord's Supper with six persons at Ramnád; and at Arasaivandai, where the Valasai Christians were now living, held a service for fifteen of them, and gave Holy Communion to six persons. At this time, there were also single families or small groups of Christians at Sakkarakottai (just outside Rámnád), Kenkondán, Pandiyur, ani Mudalúr. (3)

But from 1751 onwards the ministers or catechists who visited could find very few Christians, and on some occasions none at all. , The last worker of the Tranquebar mission who visited Rámnád was Diogo, who went there in 1762, but found no Christians. The Christians in the Rámnád district must, in fact, have practically died out at about this time. At the end of the present chapter some account will be given of the new beginnings made there some fifteen to twenty years later.

We now turn to the history of the beginnings of the congregations in Tinnevelly. These were connected not with the Tranquebar Mission itself, but with its offshoot the "English Mission at Trichinopoly and Tanjore under Schwartz, which was supported by the Society for Promoting Christian Knowledge. The S.P.C.K. had given its hearty support to the Tranquebar Mission from as early as 1709, sending out to it money, books, and a printing press; and when in 1728 the Danish Mission opened a branch mission at Madras, the S.P.C.K. undertook its' pi sole patronage and supportil, and the mission therefore became generally known as the English Mission. A second fl English Mission", similarly staffed by the Danish Mission, but supported by the S,P.C.K., was opened at Trichinopoly, when Schwartz, who had joined the Tranquebar Mission in 1750 (4) and had been able to gain the personal friendship of the Rajah of Tanjore; and had developed work in both Tanjore and Trichinopoly, was definitely posted at the latter place in 1766.

For some thirteen years previous to this, an assistant catechist of the Tranquebar Mission had worked in the district south-west of Trichinopoly extending towards Madura, and there were small groups of Christians at different places, including Nattam, only twenty-three miles north of Madura. By 1770, therefore, the Trichinopoly congregation, as Schwartz terms ity, covered a considerable area. Moreover, it would often happen that a member of this "congregation would move to some place still further off. In particular, Christians who were sepoys in the Company's forces would come to be posted at places as far south as Tinnevelly. It would also happen that a man might come from some quite distant place to Trichinopoly on business, become converted, and then return to his home, as the first Rámnád converts had done.

It was through such migrations of individuals that our Church in Tinnevelly had its beginnings. The Trichinopoly : baptism register has an entry of one such on August 10th, 1770. "Lakshmanan, a youth 20 years old, from Tinnevelly, Vellája caste - baptized as Gnánapragásam, godparents Dévanesan (a catechist) and his wife"

In the following year occurs the first mention of Tinnevelly in the missionary reports from Tranquebar and Trichinopoly, in the following paragraph of Schwartz' journal(5):

"At Palamcottah, which is about 200 English miles from Trichinopoly, there is a Christian of our congregation, Savarimuttu, who has learned to read, and reads the Word of God to the Romans and heathen there. An English Sergeant whose wife belongs to our congregation has in a manner taken up the cause. A young heathen accountant has accepted the truth; he was once here, and listened quietly to all that was shown him from the Word of God, and promised to place himself under further instruction; and the sergeant made him learn the principal Articles of the Catechismx, and then baptized him. It grioved me that he should have baptized the young man before he had attained a clear knowledge of Christianity: besides, such an ill-considered step might be a cause of scandal both to the heathen and to the Romans. May God mercifully avert all evil"

X This phrase, as used by the Lutheran missionaries, means the Lord's Prayer, the Creed, the Ten Commandments, the words of the institution of baptism, and the words of the institution of the Eucharist.

In the Tanjore Church Register there is recorded under the date of October 3rd, 1773 the baptism of a Vellala from Palamcottah, aged 18, under the name of Samuel, and at the same time his elder brother Malaiyappan, who had previously been baptized, was confirmed.

Schwartz himself first visited Palamcottah in 1778, and his account must be quoted at length. He left Trichinopoly about the middle of February,

"since I had been earnestly requested by a European to come to Palamcottah, not only to baptize several children there and at Madura, but also to marry him. The journey was, indeed, difficult and dangerous, but since a fair number of Christians live in those parts and none of us has yet journeyed there, I decided that a journey there would in many ways be useful, especially since my expenses were offered to me"

At Madura hu held a service for the Europeans at the house of the Commanding Officer, Mr. Russell, visited the great temple, and had conversations with many Hindus. On his road onwards he met a captain of a ship trading with China, and thenceforth travelled with him.

"The next day I came in the company of this captain to Koilpatti, where we both drank of a clear stream which flowed out of the rock, and both, as the Brahmins foretold, got a slight fever. The Chinese captain got it 24 hours after, I after two days. ....From Koilpatti we journeyed through forests, or rather undergrowth, which is dangerous on account of tigers. But God, protected us, so that we arrived on the morning of the next day at Tachanallúr not far this side of Tinnevelly, where there is stationed a regiment of Pariahs, who however wear European uniform. Since there are 50 to 60 members of our congregation in this corps, I ministered to them: a tent was pitched in which they could conveniently come together, a good number of Romans came also. I also examined the children to see how far they knew their Catechism.

In the afternoon we went to Palamcottah: I will shortly describe a few events there. Just as I was about to baptize some children, a young Brahmin woman came forward. With her adopted son, and asked for baptism for herself, Since the child had already received emergency baptism at his birth. I must observe about this Brahmin woman that she had previously been the mistress of an English officer soon after she had begun to live with him, she sent word to me that she was willing to embrace Christianity. My answer had been that so long as she lived in that sinful state I could not with good conscience baptize her. It may well be that the English officer privately promised to marry her, at least I conclude so from all the circumstances, as I exhorted her to quit such unclean living. He was alnost continually ill with gout, and since, as he himself told me, she gave him the greatest service, he left her the whole of his property. This officer had taught her English well, and also Bible history and the chief doctrines of Christianity - As I have said, she came forward, and said - Some years ago I requested you to teach and to baptize me, but the mode of life I then lived made you refuse me. But now again I desire you to teach and baptize me. The former reason of your refusal does not now hold, though I have not been without temptations.' Since all bore witness to her respectable life I could no longer withhold teaching from her; I therefore gave her teaching as long as I was in Palamcottah. Many Brahmins came to her, whom she openly exhorted to give up detestable heathenism. She received baptism with much emotion, and desired that she should be given the name of Clarinda, which was done. She was always ready to hear the Word of God and to join in religious exercise."

Schwartz adds that during his visit he gave three addresses to the Europeans in which he expounded the passion of the Lord Christ, and also spoke to many heathen and Roman Catholics in Palamcottah and in Tinnevelly town. On March 4th he wrote to Pohle in Trichinopolyi- ! There is a wide field here; let us pray for faithful labourers. May God send us such" for Christ's sake; yea, may He send such labourers in troops!" He gives a very brief account of his return journey, and notes that since he could not reach Madura before a Sunday, he stopped half a day's journey short of Madura, and four Christian women came to him with whom he held Sunday service.

Later in the same year one of the Tranquebar catechists working in the Marava country visited Palamcottah and reported Clarinda's zeal in preaching the Gospel to both "Hindus and Roman Catholics, and especially to women, who came to her house in considerable numbers, some from places outside Palamcottah.

At the beginning of 1779, the native minister Philip, of Tranquebar, made a tour in the South. Starting from Tranquebar on December 21st, 1778, he reached Fimnád on December 31st, and stayed there till January 12th. He speaks of conversing with Hindus there, but does not niention the Christians. Passing through Ettaiyapuram, he reached Palamcottah and visited Clarinda, and the report says:

"At her desire, he several times held for some hours a preparation service for the Lord's Supper, of which she partook with great devotion. She goes on well, and exhorts the Brahmins and other heathen and Romans who come to her, and when the native minister was there, requested him to do só also"

He visited Sharmadevi, where in the previous year there had been a very serious riot between the Roman Catholics and thie Muhammadans. He also visited the village of Puváni, near Ottarampatti, which a few years later, as will be seen, became the seat of the earliest Christian congregation outside Palamcottah, and spoke with a leading man there who was the chief manager of a Poligar.

In 1779, Poble paid a visit to Palamcottah.

"On the 16th June, I began by palanquin the journey. I had been asked to make to Palamcottah; this is my first . journey in the country, and under God!s gracious guidance I happily completed it on July 8th, when I reached Trichinopoly again."

He stayed two days with Captain Russell at Madura, and halted on the way at. Virudupatti, Koilpatti and Kayattar. At Palamcottah he stayed with the Commanding Officer, Captain Burrington,

"On June 26th a heathen of some thirty years of age presented himself for baptism. This I was not prepared for, and it seemed to me difficult to find in so short a stay the necessary time to instruct him suflíciently in Christianity. However, I asked him why he wished to be .baptized, and he answered. 1 To be saved". I also understood that he was in the service of one of our Christian women, there, so I could not absolutely turn him away. This Christian woman had formerly been the wife cfa Mahratta Brahmin who had been in the royal service at Tanjore, and was herself of royal stock, wheneeshe is called Rasa... Clarinda... She is known as a sincere Christian, and I do not doubt that she is anxious for the true welfare of her household. I have reason to rejoice that I visited her"

Pohle goes on to say that he arranged for the man to come for instruction, and found that he already knew something of the fundamentals of Christianity. On the 27 th: he held service · "in English in the bungalow of Mr. Light, the Paymaster, and on the next day baptized Mr. Light's infant són.

"On June 29th I gave Holy Baptism to the above-mentioned servant of Rasa Clarinda, and named him John: he was the first heathen whom I had baptized. His kriowledge was. certainly weak; but when I considered his candid simplicity and his great desire to be baptized for salvation, and his great distance from us or any other protestant missionaries or teachers, and moreover the uncertainty of death, I could not conscientiously leave him unbaptized. But I baptized him on the condition that his benefactress should further instruct him, in which another: Christian would assist who had the necessary books and the capacity to do: .0; both of them are the more bound to be careful in the matter since they are his god-parents."

On June 30th he married. John tóa: girl of about 18 named Mariyamm£1- whom Rasa ciarinda had inade her foster-daughter, and left Palamcottan that night.

It is, therefore, from about 1779 or 1780 that we can be a congregation o1 our Church in Palamcottah. Caldwell quotes from a register of the Tinnevelly Mission which he found in Tanjore, extending from 1780 and 1803, and gives a copy of the entries for 1780, which show a total of 40 men, women, and children, representing no less than 13 different castes. I have not, unfortunately, been able to find this register, either at Tanjore or elsewhere. But the list of names given for 1780 cannot be taken to represent accurately the congregation in that year, since the list shows serious discrepancies wit. Other information available and particularly that given by the Tanjore Church Register, which is still available. It seems most probable that this list was a copy made in 1784, with additions and corrections to date, of an original of 1780.

The next news that we have of the plamcottah congregation is in 1.783, when Clarinda and some others came to Tanjore to beg that an ordained minister should visit Tinnevelly. We have a fairly full account of this embassy, which proved to be of great importance for the future of the infant Church in. Tinnevelly, in a letter written on March 12, 1704 by the Tranquebar missionaries:

"Rasa Clarinda of Palamcottal travelled to Tanjore, just when Mr. Schwartz was away on a journey. Iwo Roman Christians who belonged to her company had arrived before here in Tanjore, and the native minister Rayappan (8) could, in the absence of Schwartz, think of nothing better than to send them on to us. One of them was a Vannárix and a well-known physician of his toWII. i had previously cruitinec a jew Testament .the : Church History printed here, (9) and as he studied them diligently had become convinced of the errors of popery, and had earnestly testified against them to his co-religionists, which had caused 3. Considerable stir which had spread too many · places. In the name of these people who were awakened and desirous of further instruction, these two persons had come to Tanjore to ask that the missionary, or at least the native minister, should go back with them.

X The washerman caste, some members of which are barber-surgeons.

After we had talked with them both separately and together, we decided to send Visuvási, our catechist in Ramnád (which lies half-way to Tinnevelly and Palancottah) to discover more fully how things stood. Clarinda had brought with her to Tanjore the boy whom she had adopted as her child (10) who had received clinical baptism at his birth and whose baptism had been confirmed by Mr. Schwartz, to give him into Mr. Schwartz charge to be educated; to this end she left him in Tanjore when she departed from there at the end of January (1784); she had stayed there a month"

Visuvási accordingly visited Tinnevelly, and on his return gave a report to the Tranquebar missionaries, which I here summarize:

Clarinda reached, Rámnád on Jan. 27th, 1784, and left, accompanied by Visuvási, on the 30th. Pitchaimuttu, the Vannán mentioned above, lived at Ottarampatti (11), where Visuvási stayed two days. Several relations of Pitchaimuttu lived further towards the south, who all recognized the errors of the Roman Chr ch and wished to come over to the Evangelical Church; at his desire therefore Visuvási travelled with him to south Travancore, and stayed for some days at Tamaraikulam, where Pitchaimuttu's brother Savarimuttu lived. They returned on March 5th to Palamcottah, where Clarinda had built a prayerhouse and appointed one Maria Savarimuttu to read services. Visuvási left Palamcottah after about a fortnight, and, visiting Ottarampatti again on his way, reached Rámnád on March 27 th.

In the mean time, Schwartz had sent his catechist (12) Gnánapragásam to Palamcottah, who, going by Rámnád, arrived at Palamcottah on March 7th. On the 22nd he went with Visuvasi to Ottarampatti; found there about 26 persons, old and young, who desired instruction; and stayed there four days. On April 19th he again visited Ottarampatti from Palamcottah, and apparently stayed there some days; on May 3rd he went to Terivilai (13), a village in south linnevelly mortgaged to Clarinda, and gave teaching to some people there. On his return journey to Tanjore he arrived at Madura on May 16th, and met there fifteen Christians, with whom he stayed four days.

Å little more than a month later, Schwartz sent Gnanapragásam to Tinnevelly again, accompanying the native minister Rayappan, who was Gnánapragasam's father-in-law; and we have a summary of the latter's report to the Tranquebar missionaries, and letters from Ruyappan and Gnanapragásam.

They were in the district from July 29th until, September 23rd. On August 11th Rayappan went to Térivilai, and on August 29t2, nine Shánars and sixteen Pariahs were baptized there. On September 3rd he went to Ottarampatti, and held a preparation service for Holy Communion on September 8th; 44 partook of the Communion, of whom 26 had come over from Roman Catholicism. He also visited Srivilliputtur, where a number of soldiers who belonged to the Trichinopoly congregation had asked him to come to perform baptisms and marriages, and he held there a Communion Service in which 63 persons joined. At Tinnevelly he mentions particularly a Roman Catholic, Devasagayam, who had a special gift of poetry. He had learnt to read the New Testament, and had discussed it with Gnanapragájam on the occasion of the latter's previous visit to Tinnevelly; now he definitely came forward. According to Giránapragásam, 79 souls were baptized (or received from Romanism) during his and Raappan's stay in Tinnevelly, the Brahmin woman Clarinda who was baptized before had some more of her household baptized; these and the people of the regiment come to 51, and so the total, including Clarinda herself, is 130. These people are not all of one place, but belong to many places lying round Palamcottah"

In a letter of February 2nd, 1785 enclosing Gnanapragasam's report, Schwartz says -

"Since it appears that many souls have sincere intentions, I cannot withdraw from the work, though the care of the congregations there will involve ne in much expense and difficulty. At present I am sending our thoroughly good catechist Sattiyanadan there to care for the congregation, which is more than one hundred strong....

"The Brahmin woman Clarinda who lives there is now engaged in building a fairly large house of stone, to which some of the English are also contributing. I suggested to her that she should make shift with the small thatched house, but she insisted that the existing prayer-house was too small and inconvenient, and begged that I should give something towards the building and encourage others to help also"

In connexion with this, we have also a letter from Ráyappan to Schwartz, written from Palamcottah, in which he says that the Commandant had told Clarinda that he would allow all stones tiles, and wood for the beams of the church to go through the fort to the church,

Schwartz had in fact despatched Sattiyanádan(14) to Palamcottah in the middle of January, and thus began the latter's long and honoured work in Tinnevelly. With him, or shortly after, he also sent another catechist, and a schoolmaster. On this occasion Sattiyanádan stayed in Tinnevelly (including the journey to and from Tanjore) from January till June. 1785, and the: following information comes from his diary:

He had many discussions with the Roman Catholics, of which he gives details. On February 4th he went to Térivilai, where the congregation had built a prayer-house and also a small house for a catechist, and stayed there about a fortnight, gathering the Christians together twice daily. He then went to Ettaiya-puram, and on February 20th returned to Palamcottah. On March 17 th he went to Ottarampatti (1f which is a German milex from Palamcottah! to visit Pitchaimuttuis people, of whom there were about thirty there...

In August of the same year, Schwartz himself visited Palamcottah for the second time, and stayed there two or three weeks. Clarinda's little church had been completed, two of the English residents having given her some financial help in the undertaking, and the Commandant of the fort having helped her with lime and some other materials. She had therefore besn urging Schwartz since January that he sbould come to consecrate it,

X A German mile is slightly more than 43 English miles; Ottarampatti is in fact a good deal further from Palamcottah. and he now did so. No details, unfortunately, are given of his visit, but the Tan," re Register shows that he performed some baptisms and receptions from Romanism, and he gives sone general descriptions of his visit in letters to the S.P.C.K. written after his return to

Tanjore. In one of these he says:

"The congregation in Palamcottah, which is about 150 strong, is hopeful. There are certainly thirty families who show a true fear of God. But the helpers there are not the men one would wish for as leaders of the congregation; one can believe that they mean well, but their knowledge is not clear, and they are elderly men and so find it difficult to accustom themselves to a well-orderea discourse. I have here two young men of about 17 years of age, whom I brought with me from Palamcottah and whom I am endeavouring to prepare for God's service."

Another letter, in which he speaks of the congregation of Ottarampatti - it is not clear whether or not he actually visited it, - shows that one of these boys was Védanayagam, son of the poet Devasagayam. Schwartz had previously thought of preparing Dévasagayam himself for the work of a catechist (he had previously been one in the Roman Church), and had had him with him at Tanjore: at the beginning of the year, but after five months had sent him back to Palamcottah, where later on we find him acting as an assistant to Maria Savari, the catechist appointed and paid by Clarinda, Vedanayagam subsequently became famous as a Christian poet, and wrote a very large number of "lyrics! or hymns in Indian metres. - Almost one quarter of the pieces in Tamil Christian Lyrics, the book of lyrics nost commonly used throughout the Tamil country at the present day, are of his composition.

In his last-mentioned letter, Schwartz writes at some Length about Clarinda, and says:

"I have most earnestly exhorted the Brahmin woman, as she is called, to be on guard against her frivolity, and have faithfully admonished her. She accepts everything that is said. to her, and if one were to judge by her behaviour to her teachers, one would judge very favourably of her. She offered me a hundred rupees to defray the cost of my journey. I did not take it, . but told her that though I regarded it in itself as right and reasonable that she should, as a well-to-do person, bear part of the cost, I could not and would not accept it, lest evildisposed persons should calumniate her as having set everything right by paying. She promised that she would behave christianly. She has up to now maintained the schoolmaster there and also given large help to the poor"

We have only one further mentions o1 Clarinda in the mission records. Pohle in his diary for 1792 records under May 13th that she came to Trichinopo]y on her way to Tanjore and Tranquebar and stayed for three days, returning through Trichinopoly after some time with her adopted son. Her death in about 1802 seems to be referred to in a letter from Kohlhoff and Horst to the S.P.C.K. in 1808 (15), in which they say:

"A Christian woman of the Brahmin caste dying a few years ago near Palamcottah, had bequeathed a considerable sum of money to her adopted son and his wife, but the money was in the hands of a rich Malabar man, and they had not yet been able to get it from him."

It is convenient to add at this point some account of the subsequent history of Clarinda's church (16). In 1818 the Rev. James Hough, then chaplain of Pålamcottahx, reported to the i S.P.C.K. that,

"This chapel is at present out of repair, though the native congregation still uses it on Sundays and the great festivals of the Church."

It was apparently repaired in Houghis time, and thenceforward regularly used as the station church for the English congregation as well as by the Indian Christian congregation, and at some date before 1826 a new and strong wall was built by the Madras Government round the churchyard at a cost of 1174 rupees. In 1848 the Madras Committee of the S.P.G., in whose ownership the church and churchyard then lay, repaired the church again at the(X **See Chapter VI below.**)Cost of 277 rupees, the European residents of Palamcottah assisting.

In the same year, however, the Government of Madras authorized the erection of a new church at Palamcottah at a cost of 3980 rupees, and the Court of Directors approved the scheme. There was a delay of some years before the decision became operative, due, it would seem, to the consideration of a suggestion that the Government should buy Clarinda's church from the S.P.G. for 1000 rupees and spend a further 466 rupees on putting it into good repair. The court of Directors, however, adhered to their previous decision of having ra church as distinguished from a room! at Palamcottah, since it was a civil as well as a military station. The building of a new church therefore went on, and the present Christ Church was dedicated by Bishop Dealtry in 1856. Part of the wall of the old Fort was removed at a cost of 817 rupees to clear the site selected for it.

0.

Finally, in 1857, the Madras Committee of the S.P.G. made over the old churchyard to the Government, on the condition that it should be kept in a decent state of preservation, and that the old chapel within the enclosure should not be suffered to fall into decay.

-

No missionary visited Tinnevelly between 1785 and 1790, but Sattiyanadan was stationed there throughout the period, and Rayappan visited the district in 1789, and perhaps in one of the previous years, to administer the Holy Communion. During this period, in fact, the Danish Mission at Iranquebar and its off shoot the pi English" Mission under Schwartz at Trichinopoly or Tanjorex had between them only two native ministers, and after Philip's death in 1788, only Rayappan. The pastoral and evangelistic work in the districts was therefore entirely in the charge of catechists, a missionary or native minister visiting the congregations only at considerable intervals. At the beginning of 1790, Schwartz reports the catechist Savariroyan as being posted at Palamcottah with Sattiyanadan, and describes him as peducated at Tranquebar; has good knowledge and a fine ability in catechizing a true Christian, but weak in health..!!

Ý Schwartz made Tanjore his headquarters from 1778.

The rates of salaries may be noted here. In the letter. Just quoted, Schwartz says:

"I give to each catechist about two star pagodas (equal to seven rupees), which is not too much; I often add something to provide them with decent clothing. To those at Palamcottah I give three pagodas monthly."

On Sattiyanádan's ordination at the end of 1790, Schwartz fixed his salary at five pagodas, which he remarks was equivalent to two pounds sterling.

We have no information of any sort about Tinnevelly for 1786, and for 1787 and 1788 only that given by lists in the Tinnevelly Mission Register and entries in the Tanjore Church Register. These show that in April 1787, twenty-two persons, including twelve Vellalas, were received from the Roman Church at Palamcottah, and that in 1788 a considerable group of Pallas of Parpanádapuram (17) was received, and a few individuals baptized.

In 1789 there was an interesting movement in the Dutch settlements of Tuticorin, Manappád, and Kulasegarapatnam. At the beginning of the year, Rayappan was sent by the Tranquebar missionaries to visit the southern congregations, and at the request of the Governor of Tuticorin went there for some months. To instruct some of his slaves and one of his domestic servants. While doing this, he also talked and preached to both Hindus and Roman Catholics; much interest and debate was aroused, and before long Sattiyanadan (with Schwartz consent) came from Palamcottah to join him. The Governor warmly supported them, and arranged for discussions to be held in his own presence; and at his instance, Rayappan often visited the Jádi-Talaivar or Headman of the Paravas and read and explained to him a booklet which had been printed in Tamil at Madras, The Mirror of Popery, and another, The Triumph of Truth, printed at Colombo. Some country-born Europeans also showed interest in the minister's preaching.

On the suggestion of a Hindu of Manappád, who was a servant of the Company, Sattiyanadan was sent there on May 4th, and soon found many ready to receive instruction. On June 8th, Ráyappan baptized at Tuticorin sixteen Maravas and eight Hindus of other castes, and received from Romanism seventeen Paravas and five others; he then went to Manappád to join Sattiyanadan, leaving those who were still under instruction in Tuticorin in the charge of a Dutch probationer for the ministry. Early in July, Ráyappan and Sattiyanadan held a large baptismal service at Tuticorin, when they baptized 226 Hindus, who included 206 weavers (Nasuvas) - 93 of Manappád and 60 of Kulasegarapatnam and the remainder of villages in the district - and 6 Shanars; and three days later they received from Romanism at Manappad twenty-three persons,including twelve Paravas.

Rayappan stayed at Mana till July 16th, when he handed over to the Dutch probationer those who were still under preparation for baptism or reception, and journeyed to Palamcottah, visiting - on the way the Christians at Parpánadapuram. Persecutions broke out at Tuticorin and Manappad, especially against the Roman Catholics who had been received or were under instruction, and he visited and encouraged them. At the end of August he left the district, visiting Tuticorin again on his way, and returned to Tranquebar, but almost immediately left again, and visited Rámnád, staying there for ten days.

It appears that opposition and persecutions continued strongly at Tuticorin and Manappad, and at the end of 1791, the matechist Gnánapragásam reported having met on his journey to Rämnad in August of that year some Roman Catholics who described to him gleefully how most cf those who had been won over at Tuticorin had been forced to recant, so that, apart from the Hindu converts, there were only some twenty-five left who could not be brought back to Romanism; the Guvernor was providing for the support of these and had given them a Dutch schoolmaster.

Caldwell, summarizing the results of the work up to 1790 or 1791, writes

"Of the converts who more or less depended for subsistence on the Dutch factories, few apnear to have maintained a consistent profession of Christianity after those factories were abandonedx

X Tuticorin was finally ceded to the English in 1825.and those did remain steadfast (weavers belonging to Manappad) who carried with them the profession of Christianity to the villages in which they went to reside, made but little progress in the Christian life. Many of their descendants are Christians still, and new converts connected with the caste are received into our congregations from time to time, but peculiar temptations and their peculiar idiosyncrasy as a caste are found to, retard their progress. Their caste is that commonly called Násuvas (properly Návitas), or barber-weavers. By prescriptive usage they officiate as the domestic priests of the Shánars at their marriages and funerals, when they expect to receive certain benefactions and dues. This circumstance gives them a direct pecuniary interest in the perpetuation of heathenism and in the retention of heathen usages by Christians; and thus tends to prevent their growing in Christian sincerity and zeal.

"There is one circumstance connected with the baptism of the persons recorded in the register, upon which I cannot forbear to animadvert. Those persons resided in no fewer than thirty-eight different villages, scattered up and down a wide extent of country, and in sixteen cases the persons baptized were solitary individuals - husbands without their wives, or fathers without their children - residing in sixteen different villages. The question here naturally presents itself - Could those persons have been duly instructed in the religion of Christ prior to their baptism? Could satisfactory evidence have been required or obtained respecting their general character or the sincerity of their wish to become Christians? And what means were, or could have been, adopted for their systematic instruction, their attendance at Divine Service, and their growth in grace, subsequently to their baptism? Considering that in the great majority of cases the converts were unable to read, and that there were not more than two or three catechists at the utmost for the oversight of forty villages, such questions seem incapable of receiving a satisfactory reply.

"In these observations, I do not attach any blame to Sattiyanádan in particular, who acted in accordance with the custom of the time, and what he supposed to be his duty, to baptize in faith all who asked for baptism and were willing to receive some preliminary instruction, leaving the results to God; but I mention the circumstances as tending to explain why the results were often so evanescent. The good seed appears to have been often sown literally by the waysidell, and in too many cases, flit was trodden down" or "the fowls of the air devoured it"

<u>RÁMNÁD AND MADURA</u>

Between 1770 and 1784, we have only slight information about the smull congregation at Rámnád. In 1771 the catechist Fáyappan was sent by the Tranquebar missionaries to the camp of the Tanjore army before Ramnad, since a number of his Tanjore congregation, who were soldiers in the Rajah's army, were there. se gives some account of the places through which he passed, and especially of Dévipatnam. At the beginning of 1776 the native minister Philip made a two months tour in the Marava country. He reached Ramnad on the 15th January, and stayed there till the 7th February, holding daily classes to prepare three Parayas and two Maravas for baptism, and baptizing them on the 4th February. il Their knowledge was according to their capacity, that is to say, only slight, but their hearts appeared to be obedient to the Ford. One was, a, woman named Annamal. He then spent a week in journey to Rämeshwaram and Dhanushkodi, and gives a full description of the island, on which, as he notes, the Romans had three small churches. As noted in the earlier part of this chapter, Philip 2. Iso passed through Rámnád on his way to Pelamcottah in 1778, and he visited it again in 1780, but only mentions conversations with Hindus.

The native minister Rayappan, also made a tour in the Varava Country in 1780, and at Rámnad held a Preparation service and received four persons from Romanism. A catechist, Visuvási, was posted at Rámnád in 1784, or perhaps a year or two earlier, end was there till 1790 or later.

In 1784, en the initiative, as it seems of Mr. John Sulivati, the British Resident at Tanjore, Schwartz began to develop a . Scheme for opening in the southern districts English Schools, or as we should now call them, Mission Schools, for boys of the higher castes

(18). He accompanied Mr. Sulivan on a journey into the Marava country and to Ramnád, during which, as Schwartz wrote to the S.P.C.K.,

"Mr. Sulivan discovered to Mr. Swartz his wish to see Schools established - observing that the English Language should be taught in such Schools, to promote the Welfare of those people, in their spiritual and temporal Concerns - that the Connexion of the Natives with the English would then, without all Doubt, be facilitated - that if some of the principal Natives could learn the English Language, in any tolerable Degree, they would be less exposed to the Imposition of cheating DubashesX - and that if the Schoolmasters should be good People, they might, by Degrees, instil into the Minds of their Pupils, the salutary Doctrines of the Gospel - The Proposal was highly.agreeable to Mr. Swartz, though he foresaw great Difficulties, in an Execution of the Plan, - The want of Schoolmasters fit for such a Business, seemed to be the most afflicting Difficulty. - However, trusting in God, a Beginning was made."

Lord Macartney, the Governor of Madras, and the Nawab of the Carnatic, approved the scheme, and the Rajahs of Ramnád and Sivaganga promised grants of a hundred rupees a month, or the revenues of certain villages. A school was actually opened at Ramnád at the beginning of 1785, Mr. John Wheatley, who had for some years worked in an English school at Tanjore, and since 1778 had been at Madras, being sent as Headmaster; and plans were made for schools at Sivaganga, Tanjore and Tinnevelly.

In 1786 Mr. Sulivan was in England, and urged the scheme on the authorities of the East India Company; he wrote to Schwartz on January 5th, 1787 that the Chairman and Deputy Chairman of the Company are become the warn Protectors of our plan for the schools, and that he had suggested to them grants of £100 for (X **i.e. commercial agents.**)Each school; and on January 29th wrote again enclosing the resolution which the Board of Directors had passed granting 250 pagogas each (equivalent to £100) to Tanjore, Sivaganga and Rámnád, and every other school which might be opened. He reported that the only material opposition had been from the fear,

"that the idea of converting: the Natives would be obtruded
. upon that of instructing them in language, and it required the
most positive assurances on my part that no such idea would be
entertained, before the objection was done away. This circumstance
coming in aid or our former opinions, will I am sure make you
particularly carefull not to suffer the most distant attempt at
conversion to take place."

He also referred to the question of a mixture of castes in the
schools, and suggested to Schwartz that is no such mixture could be
made without wc unding prejudices, one school might be confined
to members of one caste,

"Allways precluding Pariahs of every description, as they may be
instructud at the Orphan Schools by a little extension of that fund."

On the instructions of the Board of Directors, the grants : were
promptly given by the Government of Madras for the schools. at
Ramnác and Tanjore; it does not appear that the school at Sivaganga
was ever actually opened. The £100, or 250 pagodas, per year was
equivalent to 20 pag. 30 fanams per month, and Schwartz allotted
ten pagodas for the teachers and the same for the superintendents,
the balance to be used for current expenses. Schwartz wrote in
1789 that the schools consisted chiefly of pl children of Brawins
and Merchants, who read and write English, But the disturbed
conditions of the country seriously affected the working of the
schools, and in 1789, when the Rajah of Ráinad was fighting against
the Nawab, and his court was in camp for several months together,
the Rámnád school had to go into camp also, and the attendance of
children was poor.

Schwartz had visited Madura as early as 1765, when the English
army was besieging the city; he read prayers to the English and
preached to the Germans, and visited the sick and wounded, but
does not mention any native Christians, though there were
doubtless some among the sepoys. We first hear of Christians
residing there in 1778, when catechists who were touring towards
the south from Trichinopoly met at Madura four. Christians who

hai originally belonged to Trichinopoly, and held service for them. Shortly afterwards, Schwartz decided to post a catechist in the neighbourhood, since there had been very little preaching of the Gospel in those parts, and there were many Roman Christians there. He accordingly posted one Savarimuttu at Tirupattúr, about thirty-five miles from Madura and forty-five from Trichinopoly, where there was a garrison of sepoys under an English officer. By 1789, however, Savarimuttu had to return to Tanjore owing to the troubled state of the country.

It seems probable that a congregation grew up at Sivaganga at this time, or a little later, for Kohlhoff refers in 1814 to is the small congregation that was formed by the late Venerable Mr. Swartz in the province or District of Shevagunga? (20).

NOTES AND REFERENCES - CHAPTER III

1) The information about the Christians in Ramnad given in the following pages is entirely taken from the voluminous reports of .The Danish Mission in the Berichte;' for which see the bibliography. The episode of 1730 is found in Theil 3, Continuation XXXI, pp. 701 ff.

2) Aaron, the first Indian Christian to be. Ordained as a nonRoman minister, was born at Cuddalore in about 1698, the son of Chokkanada Pillai, a Vellala tradesman. Aaron studied as a boy at the Tamil Poor School established by the English at Cuddalore in 1717, and was baptized by Zieganbalg in 1718 and then given the name of Aaron. He was appointed a sub-catechist in 1719, and ordained in 1733. Theil 6 of the Berichte has a portrait of him as its frontispiece.

Diogo, already mentioned as a catechist, was ordained in 1741. He was born in about 1705, and received into the Evangelical Lutheran Church from Romanism in 1736. He died in 1781.

Ambrose, the third Indian to be ordained at Tranquebar, was born in 1709 as a Foman Catholic, his father being named Manoel, a sailor. He was received into the Evangelical Lutheran Church in 1717, ordained in 1749. He died in 1777.

3) Arasaivandai, Kenkondan, and Pandiyur are all close to Valasai; Mudalur is about four miles nearer Rámnad.

4) Christian Frederick Schwartz was born in 1726 at Sonnenburg in Prussia, and educated at the University of Halle, one of the Professors of which, Dr Francke, was a warm supporter of the Danish Mission who found many recruits for it. On his acceptance as a member of the mission, Schwartz was ordained in 1749 at Copenhagen, and before sailing for India spent six weeks in England.

5) This and other quiotations from the journls and letters of Schwartz and other members of the Tranquebar and" English Missions are translated from the Neuere Geschichte (see the Bibliography), which is also the source of many statements in the present work for which no special references are given. It has not been thought necessary to give detailed references to the Neuere Geschichte,

Bishop Caldwell in his Early History of the Tinnevel].y Mission (quoted hereafter as Caldwell) gives many of the passages in the Neuere Geschichte which are quoted here.

6) W. Germann, Missionar Christian Friedrich Schwartz, states that his name was Lyttleton, and that he was stationed at Tanjore,

7) Christian Pohle was born in 1744 near Luckau in Brandenburg; he studied at Leipzig, and was ordained in Copenhagen in 1776. He arrived in India in 1777, and after a few months at Tranquebar worked at Irichinopoly until his death there on January 28th, 1818.

8) Rayappan, the son of Andreas, whose father Marcus was a convert, was born in 1742 at Poreiyár. He was appointed catechist in 1769, and ordained at Tranquebar in 1778; he died on March 25th, 1797 at Tranquebar. A full account of his life is given in Neuere Geschichte, Bd.II, and St.21; see also Bd.IV, St.37, and Fenger, History of the Tranquebar Mission. He should not be confused with a catechist of the same name, son of Dévanesam, who died in 1777.

9) "The Church History printed here! - Caldwell notes as follows: f? The Ecclesiastical History published at Tranquebar by the Rev.

C.T. Walther, an able and learned work, written in an unattractive style: particularly rich in materials for an Indian Church History, It appears to have been the authoris principal object to furnish the Native Christians with arguments against Romanism derived from the History of the Church."

10) Clarinda's adopted son - Apparently Henry Lyttelton, son of Clarinda's servant Sarah.

11) Ottarampatti, now generally called Ottudanpatti, lies half a mile west of Lakshmipuram, a village on the road from Sivalaperi to Maniyachi, 43 miles from Sivalapéri and 10 miles from Palamcottah.

Puvani is about 13 miles E.S.E. Of Lakshmipuram; from 1791 onwards the main Christian congregation in the locality was clearly here, since the name of Puvani is always given and not that of Ottarampatti. .

Caldwell (P.17) makes a slip in identifying this Ottarampatti with the place of the same name near the Kadambúr station of the S.I.Ry, which is eleven miles further to the north

In 1937 there were about eighty Christians of the Purada- . Vannán caste scattered in villages in the neighbourhood, but only one family at Ottudanpatti, and none at Púvani.

12) Gnánapragasam became a catechist under Schwartz in 1771, and is' found working at Trichinopoly in 1777 and at Dindigul in 1800.

13) Tériyilai – "Doubtless to be identified with a hamlet called Terivilai, south of Palämcottah, in the C.M.S. district of Suviseshapuram" (Caldwell, p.17). Caldwell notes that:

"The baptism of those two families of Shanars unfortunately led to nothing. Christianity disappeared from the place erè long, and the great movement among the Shanars which has led to such important results, and which originated in 1797, was totally unconnected with Térivilai and Clarinda's people."

14) Sattiyanadan was born in about 1753, was converted in 1772, and shortly afterwards appointed as a catechist. He worked at Vallam, Tanjore up to 1785.

15) S.P.C.K., East India Mission Committee Minutes, Vol.s.61.

John Caspar Kohlhoff was the son of the Rev. John Balthasar Kohlhoff who worked at Tranquebar from 1737 until his death there in 1790. He was born at Tranquebar on May 23rd 1762, was brought up by Schwartz and ordained by him at Tranquebar in 1787, and worked at Tanjore from that time until his death there on March 27 th 1844.

Christopher Henry Horst, after working under Gericke for eleven years in the latter's school at Vepery, was ordained in 1806, and received as a missionary of the S.P.C.K. in 1808. He died at Tanjore on July 18th, 1810, aged 45.

16) For Hough's report on Clarinda's church, see the First Report of the Madras District Committee of the S.P.C.K., 1821. For the subsequent history of the church, see Penny, The Church in Madras, Vol.I, pp. 635 ff, and the references given by him. Mr. Penny, however, was under the erroneous impression that the Madras Government did not finally build a new church, and that the present Christ Church was Clarinda's church. For the final handing over of the old churchyard to the Government, see Minutes of Consultation No.321, dated 2nd Sept. 1857, in the District Collector's office, Palamcottah.

17) Parpanádapuram, which for some years continued to be one of the two leading centres outside Palamcottah, Puváni of course being the other, lies about eight miles south-east of Palamcottah, and about three-quarters of a mile south of sydunganallur railway station. In 1937 it had a congregation of 118.

18) For Mr Sullivan's letters to Schwartz, see nos.13 and 14 in the box {C. India, - Private Letters 1773-1819 to and from C.F. Schwartz and J.C.Kohlhoff!! in the S.P.G. archives.

19) In 1809 the grant for the two schools at Tanjore and Rámnad was increased from 41 to 100 pagodas monthly. See the letter from the Chief Secretary to Govt., Fort St. George, dated 21st July 1809 to Kohlhoff and Horst, quoting á letter of the Court of Directors dated 11th January 1809 (original in the S.P.G, office, Tanjore, and a copy in nos.52-54 in the box "C. India" in the S.P.G. archives:

"Having in the time of the late exemplary Missionary Mr Schwartz given our Sanction and Encouragement to the Protestant Schools established by him at Tanjore which are now superintended by Messrs Kohlhoff and Horst, the petitioners, Members of the same Mission, and being satisfied that the conduct and spirit of that Mission have proved beneficial to the Natives and tended to conciliate them to cur Government. We, in consideration of the circumstances set forth by Messrs Kohlhoff and Horst, consent to raise the present allowance of Pagodas 41 pr month, to pagodas 100 pr month for the Protestant Schools in Tanjore and Ránnad.

20) For Kohlhoff's letter, see no.80 in the box "C. India" in the S.P.G. archives.

SATTIYANÁDAN AND JAENICKE, 1791 to 1797

A second marked period in the development of the infant Church in Tinnevelly began in 1791, when Sattiyanadan returned, to Palamcottah after ordination as a minister and remained working in Tinnevelly for about fourteen years, and Jaenicke joined him there as the first resident, or at least quasiresident, missionary in Tinnevelly.

Sattiyanadan was recalled to Tanjore by Schwartz at the beginning of 1790 for special study in preparation for his ordination (1). Schwartz specially made him study the Epistle to the Romans "in order to show how Paul stated, proved, and applied to practice, the principal doctrines of the Christian religion" During Sattiyanádan's absence from Palamcottah, Savarirayan, a Tranquebar catechist, took charge there.

Sattiyanadan was ordained at Tanjore by Schwartz, Jaenicke and Kohlhoff on the 26th December, 1790, and Schwartz describes the ceremony in a letter to the S.P.C.K.:

"As the congregation at Palamcottah increases, and the. Tranquebar native dinister Rayappan is in such: bad health that. We can scarcely expect him to visit it, we have recalled the pious catechist Sattiyanadan from Palamcottah, and having given him and the catechists some preparatory instruction, proceeded to ordain him.

"His whole deportment evinces clearly the integrity of his heart. His humble, disinterested, believing walk has been made so evident to me and all others, that I may say with truth that I have never met his equal among the natives of this country. His love to Christ and his desire to be useful to his countrymen are quite apparent. His gifts in preaching afford universal satisfaction. The sermon he delivered on the day of his ordination, and his answers to the written questions given him on that occasion shall be translated by Mr. Jaenicke and Mr. Kohlhoff and forwarded to you. His love to the poor is extraordinary; and it is often inconceivable to me how he can manage to subsist on his scanty stipend and yet do so much in relieving the poor. His management of children is excellent; and he understands how to set a good example in his own house (Here Schwartz gives examples of the piety of two of his daughters)."

"On December the 26th this estimable man was ordained native minister. After the first hymn had been sung, I addressed him from 1 Tim. 4.16: Take heed to thyself!!, etc., I then received his promise to discharge his office according to the instructions that had been given him. Each of us then blessed him and commended him to the grace of God. Mr. Jaenicke and Mr. Kohlhoff next addressed him in a short exhortation. Finally, I turned to the congregation and asked them whether, as we had now set him apart as native pastor, and were about to give him his written Vocation and Instructions, they would engage to acknowledge him as their appointed teacher, and yield obedience to him? They all answered "We will". On this, I gave him his Call and Instructions; and Rayappan, the native preacher, concluded with prayer. Sattiyanadan then preached from Ezek.33. 11; and as soon as he had concluded, received the Holy Supper with us. This was a most sacred and delightful day to us all. Should I not sin to my God? The name of the Lord be humbly praised for all his undeserved mercy! May he begin anew to bless us and the congregation, and graciously grant that through this our brother many souls may be brought to Christ! Amen."

In the S.P.C.K. Report for 1791, the following note, a : worthy statement of missionary policy, was added to the short account there given of the ordination:

"How long it way be in the power of the Society to maintain Missionaries; how long the fluctuations in the affairs i of this world will afford duration to the Mission itself, is beyond our calculation, but if we wish to establish the Gospel in India, we ought to look beyond the casualties of war, or the revolutions of Empires; we ought in time to give the natives a Church of their own, independent of our support, we ought to have suffragan Bishops in the country, who might ordain deacons and priests, and secure a regular succession : of truly apostolical pastors, even if all communications with their parent Church should be annihilated."

It may be remembered that this was written twenty-two years before the appointment of the first Bishop of Calcutta in 1814, while the first Bishop of Madras was only appointed in 1835.

Jaenicke (2) had arrived in Tanjore as a missionary of the S.P.C.K. in October 1788. He learnt Tamil quickly, and in. January of 1790. Schwartz wrote that the sermons he composed in Tamil were corrected by himself, but that it was apprehended that in a short time he would stand in no need of such assistance, It was difficult to decide where he should be posted, for, as he wrote to a friend at the beginning of 1790:

"The Tranquebar Mission is wide and laborious. On Mr Gericke (5) (at Madras) a burden liés too heavy for one to bear. .. Cuddalore is without a missionary, Palamcottah is so circumstanced that a missionary there is absolutely necessary, for the best prospects are presented there for the spread of Christis Kingdom."

It was finally decided in January 1791 that he should be appointed to Palamcottah. Sattiyanádan, visiting Rámnád on the way, proceeded to Palaicottah the same month, accompanied by a catechist named Christian; but owing to the war, Jaenicke did not go till September. He first went to Rámnád, and there met a great friend of the Mission, Col. Martinz, who had formerly been an officer in the service of the Nawab, and was now in command of the local corps of the Rajah of Rámnád. . He was a Roman Catholic.

On the 26th September Jaenicke, together with Col. Martinz and Mr. Hamilton, an English official, set out for illadura, and on the 27th they arrived at Pramukkudi. Jaenicke says:

"A few years ago, it was a very flourishing place and celebrated for muslin weavers, but the oppression of the now deposed minister of the Raja of Famnad drove many of the inhabitants to settle in other places, ind the business has fallen into decay. The land belongs to the Vella or Little Maravi, or, as he is otherwise culled, the Lord of Sivaganga. The Sivaganga CollariesX plundered this place three times during the war of 1789, which has much contributed to its present decay."

While at Madura he conversed much with Hindus, twice rmed Divine Service with the English; baptized three children; and had a daily meeting for an hour with the English . soldiers. After twelve days he set out again on the 12th October, and arrived on the 16th at Palamcottah. In extracts from his diary published in his qvemoirs, and in his letters to Schwartz and his reports to the S.P.C.K. We have a fairly detailed account of his work in Palamcottah and the district during his eleven months stay there.

"Oct. 19th 1791 -- The circumstance of many of our congregation being related to or connected with Romish. Christian's causes great trouble, for it often happens that either there is no suitable person in our congregation, or else their circumstances induce persons to choose husbands for their daughters or wives for their sons from individuals of that persuasion."

"Oct. 25Th. -- I went with the native minister to Parpanadapuran, about seven miles from Palamcottah. The Christians here are all of low caste, but I rejoiced over their honest integrity, their dove-like simplicity, their love towards 'God and Christ, as well as towards one another, and their desire after the Word of God. On the 26th I appointed

X The armed retainers of Poligars, the word coming from the Kallar caste of robbers, and being applied by the English to others who were of similar type.an elder over them, Santiago, a man whom they all honour and who has distinguished himself by his piety. . I also spoke with the Headmn of the villinge, and thanked him for the plot of ground and well which he had given to the church; he promised to help us in future also.!!

"On the 9th Nov, the Colonel (Col. Clarlie, the Commandant of the Palsmcottah Fort) told me that several traders had come to him with the pretence of putting themselves under instruction. They had also been with me; but on examining them, I discovered that they were deceivers and coiners, who had cheated many persons."

"On the 28th I set out on a journey into the country. About three o'clock I reached Puvani (near Ottarampatti), and conversed with the native minister, some Christians and some heathen. The next day, after talking with Christians and heathen, we went three Niles towards Palamcottan, to a resthouse where we had summoned the Christians for a service. All the Christians came, and I rejoiced over them greatly. They live in a Christian manner and love the Word of God; Tamil avarice or other vices are not to be found among them. I asked the proprietor of the rest-house to allow Divine Service to be held there frequently, and he gave his consent; it wag necessary to do this, since they do not allow people of Low caste to be in tre resb-houses. On December 1st I returned home"

"Jan. 6th, 1792 -- In this last year forty heathen have been baptized' here, of whom I have instructed and baptized nine, three Sudras and six W ashermen.... Twelve Romans have also been received, of whom I have received six. Thirteen children have also been baptized. There were fifty-five communicants."

Jaenicke visited the western hills in January, accompanying Mr Torin the Collector, who was making a tour, and I may quote · some of his description of the scenery.

"Jan. 8th -- I went with some friends to Kalakkadu, which lies at the foot of the chain of mountains that form the boundary between the land of the Nawab and Travancore. These hills are very majestic and the country generally very beautiful. On the 20th we continued our journey, and new beauties disclosed themselves every step we travelled. At the foot of the chain of hills lie masses of rocks, great and small, many of them almost perfectly spherical and about fifty feet in diameter. The plain is well watered by streams from the hills. In many parts the grass is seven feet high, and so infested by tigers that no one ventures to travel by night, and only in company by day. After passing through an opening between two hills, we again entered a plain full of beautiful rice fields, and traversed by small streans; around were lofty hills and a second pass opening between them."

"The villages near the hills are large, the inhabitants prosperous, and the fields fruitful. There are many weavers in this district. The streans are furnished with bridges. The inhabitants are not nearly so corrupt as in other places. They are astonished at the Christian doctrines, and I saw several in tears: I trust the Lord will give us a great harvest here, if we have sufficient labourers."

"At eleven, we arrived at Ambá samudram, which contains three thousand inhabitants; the Poligar resides at a small fort at one angle of it. The houses are all good; the rest-houses beautiful, and built of hewn stone. We pitched our tents on the edge of the river to enjoy the lovely scenery; and in the afternoon, entered the town and talked with many heathen, who were very attentive.

"On the 11th, after passing through country of indescribable: beauty, we arrived at Papanasan, and beheld at a distance the magnificent falls, where the entire river precipitates itself from the hills more than two hundred feet down. The banks of the river are at least forty feet high. On the side where we were, there was a descent to the edge of the water by a flight of steps; and below were several rest-houses. There is abundance of carp in the river, all quite tame, since no one : attempts to catch them, because they are alleged to be gods by the Brahmans, who feed them with rice. The Brahmans were not pleased with our party for fishing there, and denounced. upon us death and misfortune."

In February, Jaenicke made another short trip to the hills with a party, during which,

"On the 20th I went to lenkási, a spacicus town with five thousand inhabitants. It has a large Pagoda furnished with a clock, and bell, which is rare in this country. The river Sittar flows by it.

We visited the handsome Romish church, and had an opportunity to preach the Gospel to the Roman Catholics (of prom there are about a hundred in this place) well as to the heathen."

During January and February he has the following notes of Sattiyanádan's work

"On the 31st January, the native minister and Savarimuttu returned from a journey into the country: they have visited places to which no one had ever penetrated, and everywhere held conversations with heathen. Sattiyanadan had much talk with the weavers, for whose sake the journey was principally undertaken, and who had previously intimated a desire to place themselves under instruction, they are about one hundred families or three hundred souls. But they want something done for them in which, though it is not unreasonable in itself, we can afford them no help. If they are sincere, the Lord will help them."

On the 15th February I sent Savarimuttu to Manappad get wood for building the prayer-house at Parpanadapuram, and at the same time to work among Christians and heathen."

"On February 25th I returned to Palamcottah (from Tenkási). The native minister had baptized three persons during my absence, and after I told him of the eagerness of the people to hear the word of God, expressed a great desire to visit the places where I had been. We decided that he should at least : visit some of them and remain a few days at each, and he set out on the 29th.

In March, unfortunately, Jaenicke's illness began, which continued to cripple him for the remaining eight years of his life.

"March 1st -- I was. seized with a severe bilious fever, the effect of the water, cold, dew and mists of the hills. Three of our party, among whom were Mr.Torin and Mr. Martin, the Paymaster at Palamcottah, were attacked by the same disorder. Many black people who were there at the same time died of it; I suffered a great deal, and was several times near death. On the 25th I baptized seventeen heathen and received a Romish Christian, and on the 29th travelled to Parpanádapuram to lay the foundation of a chapel"

"On the 2nd of this month (April) I was again at Parpanádapuram, and talked with our Christians and with Romans and heathen. They all promised to join us, but begged that if it were possible they should be given teaching at Parpanadapuram itself, for most of them have a number of cattle, and say that if they hari boys to look after them they could listen to teaching üuring the day and would only have to look after the cattle in the morning aná evening. I have promised them that they will be given teaching at their village,"

The native minister returned on the 2nd after an absence of thirty-four days. For three weeks he stayed with a Roman man (query, at Tenkasi), and while there, as his journal shows, was not idle. Every morning he went to some village in the neighbourhood, and he cannot sufficiently describe... the desire expressed by the people, wherever he went they begged him to read and preach to them. . He was full of joy, and would gladly have returned to them again, but I preferred that he should hold the Preparation service at Par I believe we have a great harvest in the west."

"The church in Palamcottah is too small, and I propose to enlarge it, as well as to build two chapels in the country, one at Parpanádapuram."

"April 16th -- The physician and other friends having advised me to make a journey to the sea coast for the recovery of my health, and having myself long ago promised Mr. Meckern to visit him at Tuticorin, I set off to-day for that place, preaching the Gospel as usual on the road. I arrived on the 17th, and was received with much kindness by Mr. Meckern, who is the Governor of the Dutch Factory here. The Factory is strongly fortified, but contains few houses."

"The extension of the kingdom of Christ lies very near Mr. Meckern's heart, and the Tamil Christians whom he has gathered are assisted by him in all that relates to their temporal welfare; but the care of their souls is from many causes defective. On Sundays a sermon is read to them, but there is no catechizing and no house to house visiting.. I pointed out to the catechist how he should act with the people, and frequently urged him to diligence and faithfulness.

As far as we kness permitted me I laboured among the heathens on the 17 th and the two following days I was attacked by fever and my feet were swollen."

"April 22nd -- I preached both in German and Tamil. They have no hymns in the latter language, and the Government will not sanction ours."

"24th -- This afternoon I was attacked by a severe cough. for two hours, followed by a fever fit which lasted till late at night. I afterwards had it daily till the 27th. On the 29th I attended the Dutch church, where the Dominy read a sermon; I afterwards preached in Tamil to very attentive hearers. The three following days the fever was upon me, and I suffered much from swollen feet."

"May 4th -- I visited the chief of the whole Parava caste, whom the Dutch call Prince, and conversed with him for a long time. He lives in the European manner, reads his Bible very assiducusly, and his knowledge is excellent. He would immediately renounce Popery but for fear of the Paravas. I afterwards visited the Dutch school kept by the Dominy, which is attended by more than thirty children."

A few days later Jaenicke left Tuticorin for Mana he reached on the 11th.

"The congregation here owes its existence to Mr. Meckern, and consists of three hundred persons. They are almost all weavers, and Mr. Meckern has built houses for them and advanced them money, so that they now live in great comfort; but in spiritual things they are worse provided for than at Tuticorin. Having been previously apprized of this, and of the incompetence of the catechist, I requested Mr. Meckern ito appoint a better man; it happened fortunately that there were two catechists then at Tuticorin, and Mr, Meckern immediately sent the best of them here...As the Christians have no work in the evenings, it was arranged that they should come to the church every evening to hear the Christian doctrines and to pray. The catechist is a righteous and active young man; and I trust therefore that the state of the congregation will soon be improved."

After five days, he returned to Palamcottah, stopping on the way at Alvartirunagari and Pärpanadapuran. The church at the latter place was now complete, and we have the following notes of his further visits there and to Puvani:

"July 22nd -- I delivered my farewell sermon at Parpanadapuram, on the 27 th at Palamcottah, and on the 29th at Puvani; the last was the consecration sermon (of the new church there).;

"On the 5th of August I travelled to Parpanadapuram on special business, and performed public worship there. On the 9th I was able to avert a heavy storm from the Parpanádapuram congregation. Under the government of the: Company, the Christians there had been exempted from certain State services, the Nawabis people, however, enforced those: services, they refused, and came to entreat me to speak for them. I expostulated with them very seriously, and among ... i other things pointed out that they would draw persecution upon themselves and upon all the Tinnevelly Christians, that thi chunches wo711d be piilled down and they thergselves forced to embrace raunausni suurged on then that as Niistians they were bound to set an example of obedience, and admonished them at great length. They were ashamed of their fault, and promised to do all that was required of them. On the 12th I learned that no evil would result to thera from their first refusal."

He finally left for Tanjore on August 28th, stopping at Tuticorin for a few days, where Mr. Meckern requested him to ask Schwartz to publish a volume of Tamil sermons on Christian doctrines and duties, promising to bear the expense of printing, since such a book would be of great use not only to catechists in the Carnatic but also to the Christians of Ceylon. He continued to have frequent attacks of fever at Tanjore, and was not able to return to Palamcottah till February, 1794.

We have no details of Sattiyanádanis work in Tinnevelly during 1793, but a copy of the mission register made by Caldwell (4) shows a considerable number of individuals in different villages, mostly near Palamcottah. In Sivändipatti three or four families of Maravas were baptized.

Jaenicke actually left Tanjore for Palamcottah on the 19th February, 1794, (5) and arrived at Dalamcottah on the 18th March, and remained there till 7th July, 1795. But his diary shows that he was often unwell, and could do little touring. He mentions some six visits to Parpanádapuram, and two or three to Púváni; on one occasion at the latter place.

"The Christians in the whole district assembled; they were over fifty in number. I gave two discourses, and talked with a number of individuals, especially with two married couples who were at variance and wished to separate; they become.... reconciled"

.

On a visit to Sharmudévi and Ambasamudram he found a few Christians at the latter place; he also speaks of "the Christiansi at Pánjalankurichi to whom he preached. More than once he stopped for two or three days at Attúr, and one may infer that there were some Christians, or at any rate enquirers, there.

On leaving Tirnevelly in July 1795, Jaenicke went first to Ramnad, where he stayed for three weeks, and had fifteen persons at a Communion service, and then went on to Tanjore. Sattiyanadan, who had been away from Tinnevelly since September 1794, and at Rámnád for three or four months out of that time, returned a few weeks before he left Palancottah.

Jaenicke did not return to Palancottah till September 1 partly owing to continued ill-health, and partly owing to work at Ramnåd, where a new church was being built. In August 1794 Schwartz had written to vr. Wheatley (6).

"the catechist has acquainted me with the ruinous state of the church; be so kind as to advise him what he ought to do. I shall be very happy to repay you if you lay out some money. I should think that with 20 Star Pagodasx a tolerable church might be built -- it must not be so broad; the breadth of 14 or 15 feet will be sufficientii;

and again on September 26 th he wrote to him
"At present I think it improper to pull down the church and to erect a new building. If it be covered with some straw to keep out

rain, that is at present enough. When Mr. Jaenicke returns to you, we shall then see how to go to work."

X The star pagoda was equal to three and a half rupees.

Shortly after this, however, Col. Martinz offered to rebuild the church; the offer was gratefully accepted by Schwartz, but the building did not begin until nearly a year and a half later, when Jaenicke was in Ramnad. The following are extracts from the latter's diary:

"Monday, 18th April 1796 (the day after his arrival,) - In the evening I visited Col. Martinz and Mr. Powney: I talked with the catechist and the Christians evening prayers each day."

"Sunday 24th - I preached in Malabari. In the forenoon and repeated part of the sermon in the afternoon."

"Tuesday 26th - Col. Martinz gave me 500 pagodas for the building of small church,"

"Thursday, 5th May, Ascension Day - We had two services as on Sundays. I preached on the Epistle, and gave Communion to 21 people afterwards."

"Saturday 7th - The Colonel decided on the site for the church."

"Monday 9th - We drew the line for the church-yard wall."

"From that time until the 26th August I had much work in connection with the building of the church; I also preached on Sundays and Fridays, and took evening prayers."

In the mean time, J.P. Rottler, (7) largely making the journey for his health, had visited Rámnád and Plamcottah in the autumn of 1795. He was at Rámnád from the 30th September to the 21st October and gives a long description of a visit to Rameshwaram and Dhanushkodi, part of which is here quoted:

(Having embarked at Taniturai) "the boat was paddled, and it took an hour and a half before we reached the island.o. Pámban, a small ruined fort, in which some sepoys are on guard, and which is built on the edge of the water, was where we stopped for the mid-day. The rest-house, which lies at a little distance from it, is rcomy, but not kept clean, as is the case with many others in this country. In the afternoon I set forth I had still a Kadar or more than 1 ½ german miles to cover before I could reach Rámĕshwaram itself. The road was paved with stone, since over the whole island the ground is very sandy. On both sides of the road one sees gardens, the trees of which overshadow it, and many stone rest-houses and small pagodas, some of which are especially fine, and are named after their builders..."

"On the 7 th (October) I wished to look round the neighbourhood, and cane first to the Ammankóvil pagoda, which is not far from the rest-house... The famous pagoda of the island in which Ráma is worshipped is not externally so fine as many others in the country; one tower has not been completed. It lies near the shore...!

"On the 8th I deterinined to use this opportunity to see ManaarX also, since I had hired the boat to follow me. I went ahead, however, by land to Magudarája Chattram; We proceeded along a tongue of land which stretches from east to west, on one side being the northern sea, which was very calm, while on the other side the tumultuous southern sea dashed itself. Dhanushkodi, the famous place of bathing, 13y half an hour on from the Chattram I have mentioned, and at the furthest easterly. Point of the island. I had again various discussions with the Brahmans who live there. My boat arrived in the afternoon, but since the south wind blew So strongly, I decided to spend the night there, and as it still continued on the following day, I gave up my plan of going to Manaar, and returned to lanéshwaram,"

On the 21st October he left Rámnad for Tuticorin by the coast road, and at Mapillaiyurani, an hour from Tuticorin, where the former Dutch Superintendent was living, he held Sunday services

X i.e. the island which forms the Ceylon end of Adam's Bridge. At the present day, Tälaimannar at its north-west extremity is the point of emb irkation for the passage to Dhanushkodi.for the Tamil congregation. On the 26th he left Tuticorin, and the next day he crossed the Tambraparni, much admiring the scenery, with

"The great line of mountains before us to the west, while nearer us and round us were small mountains and hills; We journeyed through a beautiful plain of rice and other fields. There were many palm trees, and there was ample water on all sides."

At Palamcottah he took up his lodging in the house belonging to the church where Jaenicke also had stayed, and found it very comfortable and in good condition. He stayed at Palamcottah until the 16th November:

"During these three weeks, I shared with the native minister Sattiyanádan in the work of the Tamil congregation, which is certainly quite as strong as that of Cuddalore or Negapatam, but is somewhat scattered. In Parpanádapuran, a village lying a German mile from the Fort there were sixty Christians, who have a prayer-house; and I spent a day with them and held Divine service.

"I went one day with the catechists Dévasagayam and Christian to visit Tinnevelly and Tachanallúr. At 9 a.m. we embarked on a woat in the river, and in less than half an hour were at Tinnevelly, which is very large, but not pleasant. I went to the palace of the present Regent, Muhammed Edubar Khan, who is generally called only Sadi Khan, and is a vassal of the Nawab of the Carnatic. He is fully seventy years old, and troubles little about the welfare of the country. As often in this country, his palace is not prepossessing."

He gives sonie details of his journey northwards:

"I took with me the catechist Christian. Towards sunset we came to the Sittar, a river with many rocks between which the water runs in smaller and larger channels, making the crossing very difficult. This time there was little water, but when it is full, it is impassable. The near-by. Place Piráncheri had so bad a rest-house that we abandoned our idea of staying the night there, and had to go a German mile further to Kayattar. There is a European cantonment there, and we lodged in the empty house of the doctor, since the soldiers had nearly all been sent off on the expedition against Mannai.

"On the 17 th...in the afternoon we went along the avenue to Koilpatti, and spent the night there."

On the 19th for the night we stayed at Virudupatti on the 20th it seemed that we must stay there, since it rained in the night and for the whole morning; in the afternoon, however, we started off in the rain, and with much difficulty got on to Tirumangalam, which I reached at about 8 o'clock; my followers, however, only arrived two hours later, the road being so bad."

At Madura he stayed for three days, and saw the sights, but makes no mention of Christians there. Of Dindigul he says:

"There is a small Tamil congregation here, with whom I had Sunday service. Since there is no church here, we gathered in the Moorish (i.e., Muhammadan) Mosque... During the singing, some Moors came in, and stayed."

As has been stated above, Jaenicke came to Palamcottah for the third time in September 1796; he stayed there till February 1797. His health was still very poor; in December and January he was almost continually ill, and on several occasions believed himself to be at death's door.

Towards the end of February 1797 he returned to Ramna, and stayed there till the 30th October superintending the church building. In a letter of 6th September he writes that the work progressed slowly owing to difficulty in obtaining materials and labourers; also the porch fell down and had to be rebuilt. He goes on to say:

"Though my presence here is indispensable in order to superintend the building, my mind has been unable to enjoy any true satisfaction while temporal occupations detain me from fulfilling the duties of my mission."

"Since 1791, Ramad has often been visited by missionaries, and six times by myself, but our residence being usually only of short duration, the real state of several of the members of the congregation was not discovered. But a short time ago, the nask fell off; and they now acknowledge that sir is the source of misery, and that to heal it lightly is the way not to eradicate it but to confirm it. I have now therefore a hope that many among them are really determined to forsake: their sins and to enter upon the only way in which we can be saved."

It is convenient to anticipate the events to be described in the next chapter by giving here the account written by Gericke of the consecration of the church at Rámnád in 1800. Jaenicke had continued to have very bad health at Tanjore, with frequent attacks of fever, and it was hoped that a journey to the south might do him good; he and Gericke therefore, set out from Tanjore on the 7th February 1800, and arrived at Ramnad on the 12th. Gericke writes:

"The 16th was a solemn day, since the church, which had been completed a year ago, was to be consecrated, and the English here had waited for us to hold the thanksgiving service which had been celebrated along the whole coast and in Bengal on the 6th of the month. The English service was at 8 o'clock. All the English gentlemen and ladies here attended the - Communion Service, after the marriage had taken place of the Collectoris sister with a gentleman of rank of the English Company's Civil Service."

"I persuaded Hr. Jaenicke to offer the consecration prayer at the beginning of the Tamil Service, since the church had been built under his supervision. He did so, but was so affected in doing it that he was seized with a severe trembling. of his hands and feet, and was obliged immediately to quit the church."

"At the Tar I service there was a Confirmation, the reception of several Roman Christians, and a Baptism. The Communion included eleven persons. One might conclude from this that the congregation there was very small; but many Christian families who belong here have gone to live in other parts, and specially at Tanjore, on account of the famine that has so long prevailed here."

NOTES AND REFERENCES - CHAPTER IV.

1) For Sattiyanadan's ordination, see Memoirs of Jaenicke; also S.P.C.K. Report for 1791: and Neuere Geschicnte. His ordination sermon was published in An Abstract of the Annual Reports and Correspondence of the S.P.C.K., 1814, and a note in. that volume states that the sermon had been published in 1792. But I have not found it in any of the annual Reports.

2) Joseph Daniel Jaenicke was born in 1759 at Berlin of Bohemian parents; he studied at Halle, was ordained in 1787 at

Wernigerode, and accepted by the S.P.C.K. as one of their missionaries in the same year. See S.P.C.K., East India Committee Minutes, Dec. 12th, 1787.

3) Christian Wilhelm Gericke was born in 1742 at Colberg in Pomerania: studied at Halle, was ordained in 1765 at Wernigerode, and came out to India in 1767

4) Manuscript in the Bishop's office, Palamcottah.

5) Jaenicke's diary from Dec. 1792 to Apr. 1798 apparently did not come into the hands of the author of his Memoirs. The original manuscript is in the S.P.G. Mission office at Tanjore, together with a translation of it made by the Rev. Frank Penny, Chaplain of the I.E.E. from 1877 to 1902, and author of The <u>Church in Madras.</u>

In connexion with his visit to Rämnad in Feb--Mar. 1794, the following list of communicants at the Tamil service there on March 9th is of interest:

The catechist Visuvási

His wife Aruláyi

Mr. Wheatleyis widow Sophia

Mr. Clarke's wife Sarah

The Liman's wife Aruláyi

The sepoy Gnanapragásam His mother Aruláyi

The sepoy John

His wife Anbayi

His mother-in-law Viyágulam

Agrorál, the wife of David Claudio

The Topaz Ignasi

His wife Jeṣuadiyál,

The Arnir Pákkiyanadan

"Topaz" was an 18th century word for a Portuguese, halfcaste, or native Christian soldier. The meanings of "Liman" and "Arnir" I have not discovered.

6. The two letters following are given in W. Taylor's Memoir of the First Century (see Bibliography)

7) Johann Peter Rottler was born in 1749 at Strassburg, and ordained in 1775 at Copenhagen. He worked at Tranquebar from

1776 to 1803, and at Madras from 1806 until his death there on Jan. 24th 1836

CHAPTER FIVE

THE MASS MOVEMENT IN TINNEVELLY, SATTIYANADAN AND GERICKE 1797 to 1805

It will have been seen that by 1797 there were in Tinnevelly three congregations of appreciable size outside Palamcottah itself: Ottarampatti with Púváni, ten miles northeast of Palancottah, which began in 1784 and consisted of families of the Pudaravannan or washerman caste, largely received from the Roman Church; Parpanádapuram, eight miles south-east of Palamcottah, dating from 1788, a congregation of Pallas,coming almost entirely from the Roman Church; and Manappad on the sea coast, starting from the movement among the weavers, there and in the district in 1789. By 1797, the numbers at Púváni and Parr nadapuram were each between fifty and sixty, while Jaenicke wrote to the S.P.C.K. in 1797 that the congregation at Manappád numbered more than two hundred, and that of the four catechists or assistant catechists who were working in Tinnevelly with Sattiyanádan, one catechist and one assistant were always at Manappad, while the others toured.

But now there suddenly sprang up a large mass movement among the Shanars. By caste-Occupation they are palmyra-tree climbers, but they have always been a community of energy and enterprise, and even at the period of which we are now speaking, many of them were owner-cultivators and some were small traders. Gericke in 1800 notes the specially strong desire of the new Christians to have schools. Both the economic position and the special characteristics of the community, therefore, favoured a rapid spread of Christianity among them, when once some leaders among them had shown the way. Nor was Christianity entirely new to them, for in certain centres there were considerable groups of Shanar Roman Catholics, though few of these seem to have come over to Protestantism during the main period of the mass movement. Only a very few individuals had so far joined the Protestant Church. Two families had been baptized by Rayappan in 1784 at Terivilai, the village in the south on which Clarinda held a. mortgage, Six Shánars of Kurugaikinaru were among those : baptized at 'Tuticorin in 1789, and one Shanar of the village of Shanmugapuram was baptized at Palamcottah in 1794.

The movement began from one David, about whom Caldwell gives the following information, obtained from Tamil letters of Sattiyanadan to the Tanjore missionaries, and from local enquiries:

"Sundaranandam, subsequently called David, was a native of Kalangudi, a village between Sattankulam and Mudalur, but the greater number of his relatives belonged to Vijayarámapuram, another village in tre same neighbourhood. As his parents died when he was young, and he was brougit up by his relatives, Vijayaramapuram may be considered as the village to which he belonged."

"In early youth he learned to read and write and versify, and being more intelligent than most lads of his class, he devoted much of his time to astrology, medicine, and magic - the scientific studies held in highest estimation by the villagers in the neighbourhood - and learned to wander about idly from place to place in the company of some philosophical vagabonds of his acquaintance. In consequence of this mode of life, he incurred the displeasure of his relatives; and one day, having got a beating from his aunt with a churning-stick for neglect of duty, unable to bear the disgrace, he ran away from home, joined himself to some travelling merchants, and accompanied them to Madura, Dindigul, and other places in the North,"

"This was about the year 1793. Ere long he found his way to the neighbourhood of Tanjore, where he attached himself to a bazaar-man, and helped him in his business; and whilst there he first became acquainted with Christianity, through - the itinerating labours of Schwartz' catechists. Subsequently the catechists brought him to Mr. Kohlhoff, who instructed him more fully, baptized him, and then took him under his care to be trained up for future usefulness as a labourer in the Mission.

"In 1796, in consequence of Sattiyanadan's application for an assistant in the rudimentary but necessary work of teaching catechisms and lessons to the candidates for Baptism and the Lord's Supper in and around Palamcottah, Schwartz, knowing that David belonged to some place in the neighbourhood, sent him down to make himself useful in that capacity. Jaenicke, who was then in Palamcottah, assented to the arrangement and David arrived in Palamcottah in September, and entered upon his duties. He was then twentyone years of age. After teaching in Palamcottah for a few weeks, and producing a strong impression in his favour in Sattiyanádan's mind, he obtained leave to visit his relatives, who after having performed in vain a sacrifice for his return, had long given him up for lost. They received him with astonishment and pleasure, and on his return to Palamcottah, he brought with him his sister's son, an interesting young man, whom Jaenicke took under his care and procueded to instruct, Shortly after this, David was sent out to Vijayaramapuram, to labour as a Christian teacher among his relatives and acquaintances in that village and neighbourhood, and the Tanjore catechists labouring under Sattiyanadan's superintendence were sent to the same sphere from time to time to render their assistance."

In a letter to Schwartz dited 10th April, 1797, Sattiyanadün gives a full account of a visit to what was already a large group of enquirers:

"On the 22nd of last month I set out to visit Vijayaramapuram, in the Manad. On my way I assembled the Christians of Patti (i.e., Parpanádapuram) and had service with them, and on the 23rd passed through sáttánkulam, and arrived at Vijayarámapuram. On ny arrival,' I began to talk with the people of the place and to tell them of the true way; and that same night began to instruct the people of David's uncle's house preparatory to their baptism. The next morning I roused them by three of clock, and recommenced teaching them the preparation lessons. During the whole day I continued talking with the people of the village; they did not allow me even a quarter of an hour's leisure, but assembled in crowds to hear the word of God. David and I were constantly employed without the least cessation in reading to them, expounding what was read, and practically applying it to them. According to the gifts we possessed, each of us so directed his remarks as to make them appropriate to each individual's state of mind."

2. We also went to a place called Shanmugapuram, and talked there for a whole day with the people.....We also went thrice to the Sáttánkulam market, and accosting the people in the outskirts of the market, where they were assembled in small numbers, explained to them the doctrines of the Gospel..."

In this manner we spent sixteen days in the neighbourhood, and David and I worked night and day. Four families were received as an offering of first-fruits to the Lord. Eighteen persons and three families promised that at the end of the palmyra season in the month of July, they would come an learn the religion. Their children have begun to learn in school. They are simple people, quite unacquainted with deceitful motives, and are all Davidis relatives. ÀS this is the palmyra climbing season, they are now somewhat hindered; were it not for this, a great number of people would join."

"These Shanars should not be treated with disrespect, but we should love them and remove every obstacle out of the eir salvation. Our catechists treated them with contempt and exalted themselves before them, and in consequence were regarded with aversion, the people mentioned this to me and complained to me of it"

"Davidi's uncle is a rather intelligent man; he has hitherto been a leader among those who practise the Saktipuja. It is the custom, as you are aware, for the pecple who practise this kind of worship to assemble once or twice a year and perform their puja at night, when they all drink out of the same vessel and all eat food together promiscuously without distir stion of caste. Fifteen houses in Vijayaramapuram are attached to this kind of worship, and they esteem it a great honour thus to have renounced caste. David's uncle was the principal man among them, but having heard the word of God, he has become a Christian and abandoned Saktipújá. When Devasagáyam catechist and Maduranayagam schoolmaster went to his house for the first time, they refused to touch even his raw rice, and went all night without food, and afterwards when védamuttu catechist was sent there, he took his own rice with him, and cooked his food and ate it by the well. When I went, David's uncle said, 'I am glad to see that you behave so kindly towards us and make no distinction of caste, but how is it that your catechists showed us such disrespect?" I answered, 'I have been ordained as a spiritual teacher to minister to all castes in common, and therefore whatever I may do, the world will not be offended at it, but the case, you know, is different with them.! He partly agreed with what I said, but added, "I hope at all events that you will visit us yourself, and that for some time to come those catechists will not be sent, so that some other people of my caste may gain salvation together with me,

"While I was thus labouring there night and day, a message was sent to inform me that my wife had suddenly been taken dangerously ill, and that I must return immediately. Accordingly that nic it, after instructing the people again and committing them to Davidis care; I set out early next morning, and by great exertions travelled thirty miles in ten Tamil hours. On my arrival I gave my wife some medicine and checked the disease. I reached home on the 7 th of this month, and on the 8th wrote to Mr. Jaenicke a detailed account of all that had happened; and yesterday, Sunday, I preached and administered the Lord's Supper"

Alter quoting this letter, Caldwell goes on to state that the first baptisms among Davidis relatives took place shortly afterwards in the village of Shanmugapuram. In Caldwell's own time it was a purely Hindu village, the Christians having moved to the adjacent, new, and purely Christian village of Kadakshapuram. Slunmugapuram has now a small congregation of some twenty Christians.

Twenty persons were baptized at Vijayaramapuram a few months after the visit by Sattiyanadan which has just been described, but when Caldwell visited the village in 1853, he could not find a single Christian there, and on learning that the first group of Shanar converts had come from that village, he was naturally grieved to think that the labours and hopes of Sattiyanadan and David had come to naught. But he goes on to say:

"On making enquiries in the neighbourhood, this melancholy supposition was agreeably dispelled. I now ascertained that the new converts, being exposed to many insults and annoyances from their heathen neighbours, and: having had their little prayerhouse twice pulled down and been obliged to assemble for worship under the shade of a tree, had at length abandoned the village where they were treated so unkindly, and migrated in a body to a place a few miles off, near the village of Adaiyal. Here David purchased a piece of land and settled his relatives upon it, built a prayer-house, and dug a well, through the help obtained from a Captain Everett, a kind friend of the Mission in Palamcottah; and as this little settlement was the first place in Tinnevelly which could be called a Christian village and which owed its existence solely to Christians, it received the name of Mudalur (First-town). The land was purchased in August 1799 in Mr. Jaenickeis name, and the population of the village at the commencement of the century amounted to twenty-eight souls. It now (1880) contains uuwards of twelve hundred."

Schwartz had for a long time approved the policy of buying Lang Lc lakin ihrisin Suoments in a letter to the S.P.C:K. of January 1786 he says that he had had the idea for fifteen or more years then. As we shall see, several such settlements were formai in Tinnevelly between 1799 and 1805.

Except for this establishment of Mudalúr,

we have no information as to Sattiyanadan's work and the progr$ss of the new movement during 1798 and 1799. But we get some information for 1800 in Gericke's account of the visit, lasting only eleven days, which he made to Tinnevelly with Jzenicze. and it will be seen that no striking developments had as yet taken place. No lists of baptisms are, unfortunately, avalible from 1796 to 1800.

as noticed at the end of the last chapter, Gericke and Jaenicke had consecrated the new church at Rámnad on the 16th Farruary. After visiting Rameshwaram, they left for the south, and Gericke writes:

"On the 20th we set forth for Tuticorin; Col Martinz. Had arranged palanquin bearers for the journey, so that we reached there on the 21st. We found here the native minister Sattiyanadan from Palamcottah, and the catechist Adaikalam from Manappad, since on Sunday next we are to baptize several children and adults and to receive some Romans, and the congregation will come here for Communion. - We gathered with them in the Dutch church, in which the preparation for the Communion, and the Baptism were held."

"On the 22nd, Mr. Jaenicke set forth early for Manappa and at the desire of the Dutch families here I preached in the morning in Portuguese in the Dutch church, and with the permission of the Dutch minister, Mr. Kluwe, aliso gave an address in Tamil. I received visits from many people, including the chief of the whole tribe of the Paravas, whom the Dutch call their prince; they all belong to the Roman Church, and the country is full of Roman churches."

"Towards evening I followed Mr. Jaenicke, and at 2 a.m. on the 23rd came to Trichendur, a famous place. After some rest there, we reached Manappad at nine o'clock, where I gave Tamil addresses in the morning and afternoon, and in the evening baptized û Dutchman's child. The Tamil congregatión there consists of from fifty to sixty families, including over a hundred souls. They live in fifty houses, which are built in a simple style of palmyra beams and leaves, and form two straight streets. The church is also made simply of palmyras and palmyra leaves. The Dutch gentlemen always attend the services, and go round with the collecting-box, SO that the congregation has gathered together a small fund. Since they are all weavers, and their wives and even the smallest children cail share in their work, there is not a single beggar here, which was a very pleasant sight for me in a village consisting wholly of Christians."

He goes on to describe how on the following day they gathered the congregation together, accepted as elders the four men whom the congregation had chosen, and set forth certain rules. The elders were to see that all men and boys came to morning and evening service in church, and that the boys attended school; the women and girls, who could not come to church while their husbands and brothers were out of the house, were to come from 9 to 10 oclock for catechizing; the girls were to learn the catechism, and the women to see that they did not forget it. On Sundays there was to be no work, and all were to come to the morning and evening services. A box was to be kept for the poor fund under the charge of the elders and the catechist. Complaints and quarrels were to be dealt with by the catechist with the help of the elders. Further rules, if needed, were to be made with the consent of the congregation. He then describes his visit to Mudalur:

In the afternoon we went five' Tamil leagues northwestwards to the next prayer-house, which, with several houses of palmyra and thatch, is on an oblong piece of ground which the missionaries had bought for eleven Porto Novo pagodas, and named Mudalur, to be a Christian village here as at Manappad. The famine, which has gone on here for two years, has up to the present hindered the building, since the good people who should have settled down here have gone to Travancore to seek a living; they are now, however, daily expected back. The people have lere the adyantage of a large square pukka well lined with cut stone which gives good water, a somewhat uncommon thing here, there is little good water to be had on all the road by which we have come from Tanjore here,"

"Early on the 25th, seven families gathered in the prayer-house, and I gave them an address, and told them of the arrangements we had made at Manappad. I gave to David, the catechist here, a young but pious and clever man, a copy of the rules which we had drawn up for that congregation, and recommended him and those families to introduce a similar ordering of affairs when all the families which belong here have returned; he should also obtain the concurrence of the native minister and of the Manappád catechist."

Gericke and Jaenicke then proceeded by stages to Parpanadapuram, where Gericke notes that the prayer-house was of stone. The leader of the Christians there, Santiago, had lost many of his cattle in the famine, and this, together with the influence of his wife, had caused him to lose his faith; but he was now repentant. The congregation at Parpanadapuram used to attend services at Palamcottah on alternate Sundays, walking in procession led by Santiago and singing hymns; on the other Sundays, & catechist generally came out from Palamcottah to hold services. On the evening of the 26th, Gericke and Jaenicke went on to Palamcottah, and Gericke held an English service and Holy Communion there on the 2nd March for siž Europeans, and afterwards held also the Tamil service. He was. not very well satisfied with the Indian congregation at Palamcottan, nor altogether with Sattiyanadan, of whom he says:

"He has great gifts, his teaching is clear and good and he is active in good works, but he allows himself to be drawn by bad men into all kinds of business in a way that injures both himself and the Christian cause. I have now laid it on him that instead of only preaching in Palamcottah and in the neighbouring villages, he should tour the whole country this side of Tanjore

We see from this that Gericke. Did not find any special movement taking place, at Muda. úr and the neighbourhood, and thought of the Mudalur congregation as simply as a fourth congregation of the same type as those in the earlier centres.

Gericke and Jaenicke stayed a day or two more at Palamcottah, appointing, elders and laying down rules for the congregation at Manappad and Parpanádapuram, and journeyed northwards on the 4th March. On the 6th they arrived at Virudupatti, and Gericke says:

"Our chief business here was to visit the Christian. Families which have moved here from Manappad, since the famine has been severe there for a year and the weavers could make no money. The catechist Adaikalam whom we brought with us from Manappad first found one family, and then all were soon discovered. They have found means of livelihood, and most of them have now no desire to return;: we therefore decided to establish a congregation here, and specially to recommend this place to the care of the native minister in our instructions to him.XX

They arrived at Madura on the 7th, and Jaenicke stayed there for some days, while Gericke went on through Dindigul and Trichinopoly to Madras. Jaenicke returned to Tanjore on Good Friday: He had taken the journey for the sake of his health, but it had done him no good, and his weakness continued to increase till he died at Tanjore on the 10th May, in the forty-first year. Of his age and the thirteenth year of his work in India.

Schwartz had died two years earlier, on the 13th of February 1798. Schwartz, in answering Clarinda's call, had planted the Church in Tinnevelly, and Jaenicke and Sattiyanadan had watered; God was now about to give the increase, though not in those congregations among whom they had specially worked.

We have practically no direct: news of Tinnevelly for the year 1801, and the list of baptists from 1800 to 1803 copied by Caldwell shows no baptisms there at all for this year. Sattiyanadan, in fact, was not in Tinnevelly during 1801. Very shortly after Gerickels departure from Palamcottah and according to his instructions, Sattiyanádan began touring over a wider area. (**XX It will be seen that two ears later they had nearly all gone back to the south -- see p.98 below.**)We hear that in May or June of 1800 he paid a visit to Pánjalamkurichi, staying a week thene instructing the Christians, and administering the Lord's Supper, to five persons;, he then went to Mapillaiyurani to meet the Collector of Ramnad, and stayed there a week, making opportunities to talk with some of the Poligars and their people who were there and to reach to the Collector's entourage and others. Towards the end of the year, he visited Madura and Dindigul and worked up to Tanjore. In February of the following year, it was intended that he should shortly go down again to Mudclúr, where a number of families who had been instructed by the catechists were waiting for him to baptize them. Just then, however, the last Poligar rebellion broke out, causing disturbances over the eastern and southern parts of Tinnevelly, and Sattiyanadan had to remain in Tanjore, and then being further delayed by the monsoon, did not get back to Tinnevelly until the spring of 1802.

We learn from Gerickers address to the Mudalur people in September 1802, which is quoted below, that the Christians there had suffered severely during the disturbances, which lasted from February to May of 1801, the violence of the insurgents. Being probably specially directed against those who, as Christians: were regiirded as hangers-on of the British. In December of that year, the Trichinopoly catechist Gnánayudam was sent, "to bring news of the mission at Palamcottah, in order that the best arrangements might be made for itry. The summary of his report which is given, however, (nly tells us that he visited the congregations, and at Kalikladu saw Captain Trotter, who was then stationed there; he was already actively interested in the mission, as also was Sergeart-Major Brown of the same regiment, who was at this time occupying the Palamcottah mission house, and who regularly took services for the Europeans and taught their children.

When Sattiyanadan finally arrived in Tinnevelly he baptized at Mudalur between the 2nd and the 19th of April 253 Shanars of Mudalúr itself and 66 Paraiyas of Attikácu, and in May and June 21 more Shanars of Mudalúr. Then suddenly the movement began to spread with great rapidity and over a considerable area, and Gericke's arrival at the end of September, was the signal for a great outburst of conversions and baptisms.

Gericke had left Tanjore at the beginning of September, and after staying some days at Dindigul to help and strengthen the congregation there, he reached Virudupatti on the 13th; here he found that the Christian weavers had all gone, or were about to go, back to the south. On the 19th he reached Púvani, where sixty persons, living in fourteen villages, formed the congregation, and on the 20th celebrated the Lord's Supper there with sixteen persons, and reached Palamcottah on the 21st. Here he stayed with Capt. Trotter, and held services on the 26th, with thirteen communicants at the English service and forty-five at the Tamil service. He notes that the Tamil congregation there and in fifteen near-by villages consisted of 105 souls(1). While at Palamcottah he received an invitation from the British Resident in Travancore to go there and to see whether Protestant congregations could be formed in that land, but decided that he had not time to make the journey.

On the 27th of September he started for the south and. Reached Parpanádapuram, where the congregation consisted of ninety persons, of whom thirty-four received the Holy Communion. He also baptized there a Chetti, who had been led to Christ by Santiago, and whom the congregation was ready to accept as their superintendent together with Santiago.

On the 28th he reached Mudalúr, and after staying two days there and baptizing some Shanars, held an extraordinary series of mass baptisms in other villages for five successive days. His own account must be given in full:

"In the evening, accompanied by a catechist, I journeyed to Mudalúr, which is entirely inhabited by Christians, many of whom, both old and young, came nearly all the way (to sáttánkulam) to meet me. They led me to their church, which is built and thatched with the stems and leaves of the palmyre tree, and which they had filled with lamps. I began the hymn, 'Hallelujah! Laud, praise and honour', and was astonished at their excellent singing. I pray ed, and then addressed them, reminding the congregation of the sufferings they had endured during the incursion of the Poligars; how the heathen had burnt their church and all their sacred books; and how several of their number had been robbed, imprisoned, and in various ways cruelly tormented, to force them back to heathenism. I reminded them also of the strength which had been graciously given them to abide faithful to their Lord; and of the wonderful increase which had taken place in their congregation since that season of bitter affliction. And thereupon I exhorted them to gratitude and to constancy in the service of Christ."

"29th from a very early hour in the morning, both Christians and heathen began to come to me, one by one, in the church, and I spent most of the day in exhorting and talking with them privately. A heathen of high rank has for several months past been constant in his attendance at the times when the catechumens are instructed and prepared for baptism; and being a man of some education, he has also learned much from reading our books. He was sorely troubled when the native minister said that he could not be baptized, but I have been obliged to confirm this decision, because he has taken to himseli a second wife, his first being childless. He was willing, he said, should he have no children by the second, to send her back to her parents and provide for her maintenance - might he then not be admitted by baptism into the congregation? But I showed him that there might be various doubts and scruples concerning this. For the rest, he has a good name amonë both Christians and unbelievers, and has sense and ability. In the afternoon I was occupied in composing some misunderstandings which had arisen between the native ninister and one of the catechists.

1930th - Early to-day I examined and confirmed twenty-one persons, who afterwards, with twenty-seven others, received the Lord's Supper. I exhorted the congregation from the words,

Seek peace and pursue it'; the subject made a salutary impression upon many, and the catechist who had brought varicus groundless charges against the native minister was so moved by it that, as soon as the service was over, he came and fell down at Sattiyanadan's feet, begging forgiveness with many tears. In the evening I held Divine Service again; the head men of two villages, who had been long under instruction, twenty-six other adults, and three children born in the congregation were baptized."

"1ˢᵗ October - After morning prayer we departed, and came to Naduvakurichi, where several Christians came to meet us, including some of those who had been baptized the previous day. I exhorted them and prayed with them, and also with the heathen inhabitants of the village. Then we went on to Bethlehem, a new village, which has also a new church, built by the catechumens who have settled here, on purpose that they might be baptized in it. They came together immediately, and I preached to them on the healing of the man sick of the palsy; and showed them the blessings they might expect from the Lord Jesus if with honest hearts they received the Christian doctrine, namely the forgiveness of their sins and strength to lead a holy life. I told them that now, through faith in Jesus, they were become pardoned and beloved sons and daughters of God. Afterwards their heathen names were written down according to their families, and their new Christian names set against them."

"In the evening they all came together again; and after preaching to them on the story of Cornelius, I baptized 203 souls in forty-eight families. Each family was called up in order by the heathen names; then the native minister read the introductory Service, and I asked them whether they now, with all their hearts, renounced heathenism, believed all the articles of the Christian Faith, and were resolved to live in obedience to the doctrine of Christ. Then the father, the mother, the children, all the meubers of each family, knelt down together, and I baptized them as one of the catechists pronounced their Christian names. In several cases it happened that the father of a family was moved to utter some very feeling words of admonition to one or other of the members of his household while they were being baptized. The service lasted from six p.m. until midnight. Sattiyanadan and the catechists said. This is like a new life to us; never has such a thing been seen in this country before"

"2ⁿᵈ. - The congregation assembled: again for morning. Prayer, after which I appointed four elders, whom they themselves had chosen. We visited several of the chief heathen men; they could not yet resolve to become Christians, but expressed their satisfaction at what they saw and heard. Then we journeyed to Náyaladi, where I held services as in the last village, and found things in the same order, except that no church had been built, for since the whole village had resolved to embrace Christianity, they had purified their idol temple and made it fit for Christian worship. These people have been instructed by Sattiyanádan and the catechists. I exhorted them from the example of Lydia, and afterwards baptized 220 souls in fifty-three families, these being the whole population of the place; after this I appointed the elders. It was now eleven at night, but we went on to Kundal."

"3rd. - The whole village waited for me to hear the word of God and to be received into the fellowship of the Christian Church by baptism. Here also the idol temple has for some time been turned into a prayer-house., I preached on the story of the jailor at Philippi, and afterwards baptized sixty-two families, consisting of 248 souls; the whole service lasted from 8 a.m. to 22.m. From there we went on to Kárikávil, where again the whole village was waiting for us, and the catechist had already written out. Their names cording to families. After exhorting them,I baptized forty-six familles, numbering 204 souls the service lasted from seven in the evening until midnight. This village consists of one long street, at the south end of which is the forner temple, now the prayer-house. It moved and rejoiced me much to see how all the inhabitants of every house in the street, both young and old, came to the prayer-house, when the catechists and the Christians from other places who had followed us here saw the people fill the building, they said Never did so many people come to this house when it was an idol temple. God is drawing men to the true Veda and to baptism.'

"4th. - I assembled the congregation once more, and after morning prayer appointed elders, and commended to the Lord the catechists and helpers whom I proposed to leave in this and the neighbouring villages, together with a young man who has been trained for this work at Vepery, Then I went on to a village called Uvari. These four villages (Sc., Navaladi, Kundal, Kárikóvil and Uvari) are on the sea coast between Manappád an n Cape Comorin, and the tract of land in which they lie is called Karai Suttu. The Uvari people had only begun to clean their temple and turn it into a prayer-house the day before, so they prepared a place in front of the emple to meet in, and were expecting a congregation of five hundred persons. But since the people had not come by noon, and my time was short, I arivised that the native minister should baptize them, or that those of them who could go so for shcull receive baptism at udalúr. The principal men of the village, however, begged me to remain and do here as I had done will the other villages.

"In the afternoon I learnt that a certain heathen, who has been a bitter enery, and during the Poligar troubles had done his utmost te persecute the Mudalur Christians into apostacy, had now done all that he could to prevent the poor people of this neighbourhood from coming to be taught. Some of them, however, whom he could not deter by either his threats or his promises, arrived, and begged that I would stay with them till the next day. In the evoning. I preached on the parable of the Sower, and was well satisfied with the attention of the people."

"5th. - All this day was spent in teaching the people, amongst those who came to me was a man in the custody of two sepoys. He had been attending regularly to receive teaching from the catechist before he was arrested on the charge of having been concerned in the plunder of a village three years ago, and he was now undergoing imprisonment for this crime. But he begged to be baptized, saying that he had learned much of our doctrines by reading books during his imprisonment. I preached to-day on the parable co the Tares and the Wheat, after which twenty-three families, consisting of 102 souls, were baptized. It was two hours after midnight before I could take any rest."

On the 6th, Gericke went on to Taruvai, where there were a number of catechumens who were going to Mudalúr for teaching,

He stayed there an hour or two, and then went on to Padukkapattu, where the headman of the village wished to become a Christian when the body of the villagers would come with him, and went on in the evening to Manappád. Here he found the congregation ron the whole in not so satisfactory a condition as they were about three years ago, when that judicious and faithful catechist. Adaikalam was their teachers. On the next day Sattiyanádan and the catechists followed him from Padukkapattu, bringing word that fifteen of the people had resolved to follow the headman, and were ready to go to Mudalúr for teaching, and had asked for their names to be written down; they were all of the high caste of Vellalas"

The congregation at Manappad now numbered 113; it had been larger in 1800, but many had since gone to Ceylon, where there was a demand for weavers to start the industry there. On the next day Gericke held services in the Dutch church at Manappad both for the two Dutch families there and for the Tamils, and in the evening came .on to Trichendur, where he met the Collector of the Marava. Country, i.e. Rámnád, whose interpreter and clerk was William Wheatley, the adopted son of the Rannad schoolmaster (2). He introduced Sattiyanáden to the Collector, and spoke to him about the troubles which the Christians at Uyari had suffered; he also spoke with one Lala Sahib! A high caste Hindu. From - Benares who held charge of the sub-district under the collector, and urged him to be friendly to the Christians; he was courteous. On the 14th evening, Gericke left Trichendúr and travelled to Pallipattu, and writes:

15TH the Here I have bought a piece of land for a new Christian village and a church for thirteen families, altogether forty eight souls, who belong to different villages, round here. They have for some months been going to mudalúr for teaching, and were baptized to-day in a pandal on the site where the prayerhouse will be built."

This Christian colony was named Jerusalem. Gericke found a catechist for them and a schoolmaster in the person of the Hindu schoolmaster of the place, who was among those baptized.

Gericke then went to Tuticorin, where he stayed for a day, and then travelled northwards, reaching Rámnád October and leaving it on the 24th; at lis service at Ramnád he had six English communicants and fifteen Tamil, of whom six were newly confirmed.

It is seen from Gerickers account, and from the detailed figures given in the baptism lists copied by Caldwell, that between the 1st and the 6th of October he baptized 977 persons at, five villages - Achampádu (or Bethlehem), Navaladi. Kundal, Kárikóvil, and Uvari. After his departure; Sattiyanadan continued the work, and in November and December baptized 3057 more persons in South Tinnevelly, nearly all of whom were shanars. These included groups of over 150 each in Navaladi (934), Idaiyangudi (311) Anaigudi (249), Lakshmipuram (168), and Avudaiyapuram (157). The conversions and baptisms then seems to have ended, though, as we shall see, there continued to be appreciable accessions during the next three years.

The persecutions, which immediately arose against the Christians were coilsiderable, and may 12:17e contributed to the showing cowl of the movement. Not only did the Hindu leaders persecute them in various ways, but the suvordinate officials, who were of course Hindus, extorted unauthorized taxes from theidanů made complaints : against them to the Collector. Such troubles began even before Gericke's visit to Tinnevelly in September/ October 1802, and matters were made worse by the action of the catechist David, who put himself at the head of a body called club- men, which went about from place to place attempting to redress the wrongs of the converts by force. Shortly after his return to Madras, Gericke wrote on November 23rd to Mr. Lushington, the Collector of Tinnevelly, enclosing a petition which he had received in several months ago from the Christians of Mudalúr and Manappad, and writing:

"I am informed that the Chetties mentioned in the petition, insteacł of giving the poor people any hopes that they shall not be molested by them hereafter, exact more from them than what they have a right to demand, and what they demanded of them befcre the late troubles gave them an opportunity to treat them so ill.. The Christians of Mudalur have heretofore paid what, agreeably to the writing by which that place was conveyed to the Missionaries of Tanjore, the inhabitants have to pay, but now another tax is demanded of them, and the poor people are afraid that the Chetties will carry on their oppressions to still higher degrees; seeing that nothing is done for their relief, who suffered more by them than by the war. This has induced me at last to lay their complaint. Before you...."

A letter from Mr. Lushington dated 4th December must have crossed this. Mr. Lushington forwarded a complaint from a Tahsildar, and wrote that he had directed Sattiyanádan not to receive any of the Maravas into the congregation, is for they wish to make use of a species of protection which I have hitherto allowed him to exercise, for purposes of conspiracy and disturbance." He requested Gericke to direct Sattiyanadan to hold no intercourse with men of So immoral character as the Maravasil, and to abstain from all interference in the temporal concerns of the newly converted Shánars.

Gericke answered on the 15th December that while his own knowledge of the facts make him discount a good deal of what the Tahsildar had said, he had found that one of the catechists had been i meddling with things with which he had no business, and would have dismissed him if the shortage of catechists and schoolmasters for so many congregations had not obliged him to keep him in the service of the Mission on trial.

Gericke does not refer in this letter to the question of receiving Maravars into the congregations, but on the 22nd December he wrote to. Sattiyanadan as follows:

"It is impossible for me to return immediately to Tinnevelly as you ask in your letters, though I am very desirous of doing so. Accordingly, Mr. Kohlhoff will come instead and will try to bring all things into order. I am very sorry that the Maniyakaran Adaikalam has suffered so much Iron Lalax and his people, assure him that I suffer with him. I am surprised that they should have treated him in this (X i.e., the "Lala Sahib" mentioned above.)way, though he had faithfully paid what was due to Government even before the fixed date. If you will let me know the cause of this, I will write about it to the Collector."

"I am glad to find that, in accordance with the Collector's letter to you about the Maravars; you have not received them - into the congregation. The Collector wrote to me that it was not proper for the native minister to be intimate with those wicked people; this is true. The Lord calls both the good and the evil; not that He may fill his house with the evil, but that He may make the evil good. If those Maravars are disposed to become good, they will be received in due time; you have now an opportunity to encuire about them and to keep them under probation."

"In accordance with the Collector's second letter to you, it will be desirable that neither you-nor any of the catechists should interf're in any matters connected with the Government. If the Government officers find us doing so, they will be irritated, and also the ryots will be tempted to disobedience. If, however, any persons are unjustly treated by the Governient officers in consequence of their having become Christians, send me information about it with sufficient evidence, and then I shall be able to render what help I con in the matter...."

Kohlhoff paid the promised visit to Tinnevelly in the following spring, and he gives some account of it in a letter to the S.P.C.K. of March 1805. He expresses his gratitude to the Collector at Palomcottah for the consideration he had shown to the representatives of the Christians, and goes on to say that the orders issued by the Collector had considerably checked the persecution of the Christians; but that the Mudalur church had been burnt on the 22nd May 1803. The incendiaries, however, had been arrested, tried at the Sessions, and punished with flogging and seven years imprisonment with hard labour. This last news he had received in August, after his return to Tanjore. His letter i continues:

"After finishing iny business at Palamcottah, I visited all the congregations in the Tinnevelly country, and was sorry to find that in five different villages the greatest part of those who had embraced Christianity had proved unfaithful! to their Christian engagements, in consequence of the persecution ihey had met with; but it was great joy to me that all the other congregations were firm in their Christian profession and not afraid or ashamed to confess the name of their blessed Redeemer under trials and sufferings. I exhorted thein."

"In most of the congregations I was received with great joy, which they especially showed by their cheerful attendance at the hours of instruction. They gladly received the word of God preached to them, and promised not only to act according to the same, but to the instructions which were given for: their regular attendance at Divine Service on Sundays and the sending of their children to be instructed. In my visit to the new congregations I have baptized 108 catechumens who had been previously instructed and had a competent knowledge of the doctrines of Christianity, and administered the Lord's Supper to 138 persons."

"In my journey to Palamcottah, as likewise on my return, I visited the congregation at Rámnád, where I found the congregation but small and in the same state as it was when the late Rev. Mr. Jaenicke resided there. I preached several times in the new chapel built by him, administered the Holy Sacrament to fourteen persons of the Tamulian congregation, and baptized the child of a European officer,"

Gericke died at Vellore on the 2nd Üctober 1803, and Kohlhoff at Tanjore had henceforth full supervisory charge of all the southern congregations as well as those round Tanjore and the . charge of the new English garrison at Tanjore, and found himself unable to visit Tinnevelly again, Sättiyanadan, however, ramained in Tinnevelly until August 1805, and made regular reports to Kohlhoff. He gives the following list of baptisms in Tinnevelly for 1803:

Mudalúr 37

Pottakulam 24

Uvari 9
Kundal 21
Pudiír 35
Nandankulam 17
Idaiyangudi 22
Bethlehem 19
Ánaigudi 17
Marakáttuvilai 17
Návaladi 27
Changudi 6
Appuvilai 13
Attiladu 15
Total 279

In December 1804 he writes to Kohlhoff:

"I spent twenty days in Pallipattu (Jerusalen), held a Preparation service, and baptized thirty persons. From thence I went to Valaiyadi, settled some disputes there, and baptized twenty-five people. I went thence to Mudalur, then to Bethlehem, and from thence to Uvari, where I dedicated the church built by Kailasa Nadan Then I visited Idaiyangudi and Sotakaivilai, and dedicated a new church at Appuvilai, which had been built by the people in place of the one which the heathen had destroyed. I dedicated also a church at Niittuvagai, and then went to Manappad on account of an affair which had taken place there; the Maneppád Christians were reported to have subscribed 18 fanams a head for the completion of the idol car at Trichendúr. On enquiry I found the report confirmed; I put the affair in Mr. Gratianis hands, and they confessed their fault and asked me to dismiss them from the congregation. I assembled them all in church, rebuked them everely, inade an arrangement for their future good behaviour, made them over to Palkiyanadan catechist, and then returned to mudalur.

"On returning to Müdülúr I sent Yesadian catechist into Travancore. After he had been there four days it came to be known that the native authorities had imprisoned Major MacaulayX, whereupon the Christians sent Yesadian back into Tinnevelly, saying that any person sent into Travancore by the English and found within the gates would be arrested and imprisoned. Yesadian reported that the Christians in Travancore were good people, and that labour expended in that country would not be in vain, but that one must refrain from doing anything further just then.(X **This was a false rumour**)

"I have received no money for the Mission since October, and the people are pulling mc to pieces for their salaries; besides, everything just now is very dear and everybody is suffering from the scarcity."

Sinnamuttu catechist itinerates to the north of the river and locks after the people at Eral, Nattátti, and Sirutondu. I have placed a catechist in each of the three villages oí Kundal, Kárikóvil and Marakattuvilzi, and since Pudúr is a large place, I have a schoolmaster there, as well as Mengnanam catechists who has also charge of Marakundal."

He adds in a postcript: "The Válaiyadi people are suffering a great deal of trouble. Swamidása Nadan is coming to Tanjcre to tell you all the particulars."

He gives the following list of baptisms for 1804:

Mudalúr 20

Attikádu 3

Kárikovil 40

Pudúr 20

Jerusalem 35

Nazareth 39

Idaiyangudi 24

Kundal 3

Total 184

In January 1805, Sattiyanadan wrote another letter to Kohlhoff, in which he says that there were thirty-five communicants in the new church at Mudalur on Christmas Day, and fifteen on New Year's Day, and also gives a full list of the country. Congregations outside Palimcottah, numbering thirty-four, a summary of which

I print in Appendix A. This list is clearly only Intened to include settled congregations. at which a catechist or assistant was stationed, or which were regularly visited by a catechist, and each Village mentioned must be taken to include small groups of Christians living near by. Some twenty-six churches or prayei -houses are shown, and eleven schools. He also speaks of two new openings to the south-west and north-west respectively of the central grou) of villages near Idaiyangudi:

"In adlition to all this, five people have cone from Kúa nkulam, and have been waiting here vight days, entreating me to visit their village. Also onë Muttaiya Nadan of Parpadi has pulled down the devil-temple in which ne formerly worshipped, his procured books which he reads himself, and has sent two of his people to me urging me to come and help him. All this is a burden beyond my strength. I shall inform you afterwards what happens there. Also it appears that Travancore has passed into the Company's possession, and the poor Christian people there urging 111€ to come and visit them."

It will be seen from the above that from 1803 to 1805, Sattiyanadan's work was mainly one of consolidotion, though converts were also appearing in some new villages. Those at Eral, Nattáttis and Sirutondu, north of the river were the beginnings of the large congregations in the present Pannaivilai and Sawyerpuram circles; we also note the beginning of Nazareth, which has for many years: been the largest Christian centre in Tinnevelly outside Palancottah. The first baptisms recorded at Valaiyadi were in October 1802, and a group of twenty-three Shanars was baptized in June 1803, and Nazareth seems to have sprung up very soon afterwards as a settlement just outside Valaiyadi. Caldwell notes:

"From the first it was called Nazareth in all Mission correspondence, but the nme válaiyadi. Mudulur, that is, the Mudalúr adjacent to valaiyadi, by which it came to be generally called by the common people, must have come up at an early period. This double name came, in the northern parts of Tinnevelly, to be abbreviated into udalúril, and then in order to distinguish it floin the real Mudalúr, the latter came frequently to be called South

Mudalur."

Another completely Christian settlement to be noted is that of Samaria, on the outskirts of the town of Tisayanvilai.

Throughout 1804. and 1805 the Christians continued to be troubled by persecutions and unjust exactions by the minor Hindu officials, of which Kohlhoff's letter of March 1805 to the S.P.C.K. .

X This was a false rumour, arising from the fact that at that time there was tension between the Travancore government and the Company with regard to a proposed new treaty.

Gives various examples, and also shows that the Collectors (Mr. Cochrane succeeding Mr. Parish in 1804), while sharply on the look-out lest the Christians should in any way presume on an imagined position of favouritism, were ready to sift any alleged case of persecution or injustice and to punish severely those who were found guilty. The Christian Knowledge Society also took the matter up on Gerickers and Kohlhoffis reports and made representations to the Court of Directors of the Company, who sent out to Madras an important order on the subject, which, as Caldwell remarks, of constituted the first official recornition by . The East India Companyis Government of the propriety of extending to Native Christians the religious toleration which it had always been more than willing to show to Hindus and Muhammadansit). In this order, after stating that the representations received from the S.P.C.K. had not been in the least intended to reflect on the European servants of the Company, and recognizing the strong action that had been taken by Mr. Lushington to stop injustice committed against Christians, the Directors went on to say:

"Satisfied that there has been no intentior. in our Government to act otherwise, we think it requisite only to stite, that as we have never countenanced any species or degree of religious intolerance in the countries subject to our authority, and Mahomedans, Parsees, Hindoos, in all their varying sects, have been permitted to follow their separate persuasions without molestation, so it can be no question that all who profess the Christian faith, whether of Euri pean, Armenian, or Indian race, should enjoy the like privilege and protection. Therefore officers of every rank, Europeans and Natives, employed in the administration of our affairs, should conform themselves to these general principles, from which any deviation past or future might excite our disapprobation, and whilst those officers are careful to secure the obedience, and the revenue due to Government, they should be the defenders of every subject against injurious treatment on a religious account... With regard also to the Missionaries, so long as they conduct themselves in a prudent and upright nanner, as they!ppear hitherto to have done, we cannot doubt that their persons and office will be duly respected."

Sattiyanadan was recalled to Tanjore in August 1805 at his own requesting in consequence, Caldwell says, or misunderstandings that had arisen between him and Kohlhoff. Mr. Sawyer, an East Indian or Portuguese merchant in Palamcottah, was a good friend of the mission, and acted as Kohlhoff's financial agent, negotiating bills for the mission and sometimes: advancing money. But, as Caldwell reports from the correspondenc --- which he had seen,

"There seem to have been two parties in the Mission: that time, the: Tanjore party headed by Sattiyanådan, and

The locul Shanar party headed by David Catechist of Mudalur The latter party wished it to be supposed that they were: favoured by Sawyer and made much use of his name. On the other hand the Tanjore party endeavoured to lower Sawyer in Kohlhoffls estimation".

It may be noted here that Schwartz, in spite of a very hi regard for Sattiyanadan, had found some weaknesses in him. In a letter to Mr. Wheatley of Ráminåą in 1795, he wrote:

"Your regard for Sattiyanadan, the country priest, is very pleasing. Be sure that none has ever esteemed him so inuch as I have done. His preaching is edifying, for his knowledge is competent. But in humility he is deficient, and therefore to those that are under him over-bearing, which has caused great complaints against him. His indulgence to his children is extravagant, by which he has spoiled them. His daughter has been married to a pious catechist.

I will not say that she despiseth her husband, but to his mother, brother, and sister, she will not show even common civility; by which she has lost their regard. The father observes. This, and is grieved; but, instead of rebuking the agughter, he follows her example. I have frequently intreated him to shew kindness to those people, considering that his son-inlaw will not abandon his mother and relations for his wife's sake. Having a mind to preserve peace: betwixt both, I suffer by these animosities."

After Sattiyanadan's return to Tanjore, however, Caldwell says that the friendly relations which formerly existed between Kohlhoff and him seem to have been restored. He continued to work at or in the neighbourhood of Tanjore until his death in 1815, at the age of about 57, and we have only record of his paying one visit to Tinnevelly in 1810, Tinnevelly may well hold his name in high honour among the fathers of its Church. As catechist and minister he worked there for nearly twenty years, far longer and more continuously than any missionary until Rhenius, and saw the development of the Church from two small congregations in Palamoottah and Ottarampatti to a body of several thousand members in some thirty-five centres. It was not until John Dévasagayam began his ministry in Tinnevelly in 1832 that any Indian minister of at all the same spitirual and mental power was found to succeed him. Caldwell writes of him:

"On account of the lateness of his conversion and his want of a Christian education in his youth, his acquirements were not equal to those of some of the native preachers who succeeded him in Tinnevelly; but all accounts agree in representing his name as the first in the line as regards character as well as in the order of time, He is universally described as having been a man of true Christian integrity; of remarkable generosity; simpleminded, but earnest and fearless; impressive in his manner of address, and somewhat inclined to be authoritative in his modes of procedure. On the whole it may safely be concluded that his general style of character was well adapted to the nature of the work oommitted to him by

Providence - that of laying the foundation of a Christian Church among a rude and illiterate people,"

Kohlhoff had no ordained minister whom he could send to Tinnevelly (4) to take Sattiyanadan's place, but sent a catechist in whom he had confidence, Gnánapragásam, to superintend the Mission, instructing him always to consult Sawyer, and requesting Sawyer to help him with his advice. Gnánapragasan unfortunately appears to have joined what was described above as the Tanjore party in Tinnevelly and to have set himself against Sawyer.

We have no information about his work except that which may be inferred from the baptism lists (5) which show apreciable groups of converts baptized towards the end of 1805 and in the beginning of 1806 at Jerusalem, Mudalúr, and Atti adu. Kohlhoff was also at this time endeavouring to arrange for Ringeltaube, whose work in Tinnevelly will be described in the next chapter, to come to Palamoottah, and in September of this year (1805) gave orders that a house should be prepared for him there.

RÅNÁD, MADURA, and DINDIGUL

Apart from the visits made in passing by Gericke in 1802 and Kohlhoff in 1803, we have no information about Ramad during the period covered by this chapter subsequent to the consecration of its church in 1800. Of a regular congregation in Madura we hear Pirst at the end of 1800, when Sattiyanadan visited it; and February 1801 Gericke wrote to the S.P.C.K. that a chapel was about to be built there. We also hear of the catechist Gnanayudam visiting the Madura congregation in March 1804.

Of Dindigul, where the congregation seems to have been distinctly larger, we have a fair amount of news, as it was visited by catechists from Trichinopoly two or three times a year. In December 1798 the catechist Gnanayudam found a congregation of fifteen adults. He stayed there for about three weeks, the regimental store-keeper giving hin a room in which he could gather the Christians. During the next two years, the little group succeeded in building a prayer-house for themselves, and though it was not quite completed, Gnanapragasam held service in it in July of 1800,

In December of that year, the congregation numbered seventy-one souls, Sattiyanadan having baptized and received some who had been taught and prepared on previous visits by catechists sent by Pohle.

On his journey in the autum of 1802, Gericke stayed for some days at Dindigul; he baptized eight adults there, and held a Holy Communion service with 29 persons, and also an English service for the Collector, the officers, and other Europeans. There was a Brahman there who taught English to the European children; he had an English Bible and some good primers, and Gericke added some alphabet books, catechisms, Dr. Watts! Hymns for Children, and a rżyer-book, also some Tamil books...

On the catechist Gnánayudam's visit in February 1804, the girrison had left Dindigul, and the congregation numbered only 55. In December of that year he found that the prayer-house had collapsed in the rains, and had not yet been rebuilt; the Christmas congregation numbered 22 Portuguese' and 28 Malabarsfi (i.e., Tamil Christians). In the following December (1805) the numbers were respectively 8 and 33.

NOTES AND REFERENCES - CHAPTER V

1) While at Palamcottäh, Gericke baptized among other adults. la Maravar of 27 years, whose father became a Ch years ago. The father is a poet, and has made a number of hymns in praise of the Lord Jesus. The name is unfortunately not given.

2) William Wheatley was clerk to the Tinnevelly Collector from a date some years before 1802. W. Taylor in his Memoir gives a number of letters to him from Schwartz, Jaenicke, and Gericke, and Caldwell (2.97) gives a letter to him from Gericke which shows that in 1801 he was acting as agent for the Mission in Palamcottah.

3) For the full text of the order, see Caldwell, p.119.

4) Between 1797, when Rayappan died, and 1811, when Gnánapragásam and Adaikalam were ordained, Sattiyanadan was the only native minister in the Danish and S.P.C.K. missions. In 1806 the missionaries were:

At Tranquebar - Ch. S. John (then old), A.F. Caemmerer, ana D. Schreyvogel (then a lector, or catechist); at Tanjore, Kohlhoff and C.H. Horst (ordained in 1806, previously a lector: at Trichinopoly, Pohley at Cuddalore, I.G. Holzberg; and at Madras, C.W.Paezold. J.P. Rottler was also at Madras, but at that time unconnected with any mission.

5) The lists for 1805 and 1806 are in a paper book in the S.P.G. Mission office at Tanjore,

CHAPTER SIX

RINGELTAUBE IN TINNEVELLY, 1806 to 1808: FEVER AND FAMINE, 1808 to 1816.

William Tobias Ringeltaube (1) arrived at Tranquebar early in December, 1804. He had gone to Calcutta as a missionary of the 9.P.C.K. in 1797, but in the following year had returned to Europe, stating that his allowance was inadequate to his support and that he saw no prospect of usefulness there. In 1803 he was accepted as a missionary of the London Missionary Society, which had been founded in 1797. The Society had been invited by the Danish missionaries to take up work in the Tamil country, and resolved that Ringeltaube

"Should proceed as soon as it may be practicable to the Coast of Coromandel, with a view to act as a Missionary on that Continent or at Ceylon, as may hereafter appear most. Desirable after consultation with Mr. Gericke."

Two other new missionaries, Cran and Desgranges, sailed with him in 1804. Shortly after their arrival at Tranquebar, they decided to go and work at. Madras; but Ringeltaube, thinking, as he said in a letter some months later, that if The Missions. cannot be so well carried on in great towns where Europeans reside, as they some times counteract the pious labours of the Missionaryit, thought rather of the south, and already at the end of January 1806 was proposing to go to help the congregations in Tinnevelly which, as he had heard, begin already to disperse for want of a shepherd. In April he wrote to Mr. Gratian of the Dutch factory at Manappád, which he had heard of as a promising station; Mr. Gratian answered him, and in a second letter of June 8th to a mutual friend urged him to come as soon as possible, since the Christians were suffering severe persecutions. The catechist of one village had been forced to flee to Palámcottah,

"whilst the exasperated mob, coming from Padukapattu, hovered round the village plundering the houses of the Christians, and ill-treating their families by kicking, flogging, and other bad usage; these monsters not even forbearing to attack, strip, rob, and miserably beat the catechist Yesadian, who partly from illness and partly through fear had shut himsel, I up in his house."

About the same time, however, Ringeltaube. Received a call from Travancore which greatly impressed him. A Paraiyar of the village of Mayiladi in South Travancore, named vedamanikkam, while visiting the great shrine of Siva at Chidambaram, became deeply disappointed at finding the holy place full of worldliness, and saw in a vision one who rebuked him for coming there and bade him return home. On his way home he stopped at: Tanjore, where some of his relatives lived who had become Christians; they brought him to Kohlhoff; who gave him teaching and soon baptized him. He then returned to his home and began to try to convert his relatives and neighbours, but he and a group of his relatives who followed him met with opposition and persecution, and he again resorted to Tanjore to obtain Kohlhofft s advice. He arrived there at the time when Ringeltaube was considering going to the south, and Kohlhoff sent him on to Tranquebar to see Ringeltaube.

Ringeltaube finally decided to take up the work in Tinnevelly, and, it would seem, to combine with it some work in Travancore. Writing to the London Missionary Society on October 4th, 1805, he gave a general description of the South Tinnevelly field and gave hopes that Mr. William Wheatley would be able to join him as his assistant, putting forward the following proposals:

"If the Society should be willing to take the whole Mission in the Tinnevelly district under their wing, the annual expenditure would be as follows:

TO Ringeltaube £ 100

To Wheatley £ 100

To Thirty catechists £ 300 £ 500 per annum.

"There are already said to be five thousand converts in Tinnevelly, accordingly the annual expense of our Society for the good of one of these would be 2s. 4d"

"There is a reasonable hope that the number of converts would increase from the moment of a Missionary's arrival among them. I should think, indeed, that if the Society undertook the concern, I might be under a necessity of discharging perhaps one-hall of the catechists as unconverted men. This would prove a great reduction in the expense. I also think that in time, the number of catechists might still be diminished, and in the stead of them, a few travelling preachers might sustain their office, whilst the most pious persons in every flock might act as leaders and exhorters."

"Upon the whole, however, is the society thinks the Tinnevelly Mission would be upon too expensive a plan, is it their will that I should continue to reside in some part of that province, and begin a little Mission of my own? What idea strikes them in such a case as most proper to be acted upon? To enable them to discuss this question with more propriety, I shall give our Directors more ample information in future communications."

The Directors of the Society largely accepted Ringeltaubels immediate plans, but were cautious as regards the idea of taking over the whole Tinnevelly mission, and resolved on 30th June 1806

"That under a conviction of the vast importance of furthering the Mission in the Tinnevelly Country, described in Mr. Ringeltaube's letter dated 4. Oct. 1805, he be authorized to employ Mr. Wheatley or another person on an annual allowance not exceeding £100,"

"Mr. Ringeltaube having suggested the propriety of taking the whole Mission in the Tinnevelly District under the patronage of the Society - this subject appearing of so much importance as to render it desirable to obtain more full information from him - and in the mean time he be given £100 with authority to engage catechists or travelling preachers or to adopt other measures."

Bishop Caldwell states that he had received personal information from Kohlhoff about the circumstances of Ringeltaubels going to Tinnevelly. Being quite unable himself to give any practical superintendence to the congregations in the extreme south, he agreed with Ringeltaube that while the latter endeavoured! to establish a mission of his own in Travancore in connexion with the London Missionary Society, he should also take temporary charge of the S.P.C.K. mission in Tinnevelly in Kohlhoff's name and on his responsibility. Since Ringeltaube, like Kohlhoff, was in Lutheran orders, Kohlhoff felt confident that he would manage the affairs of the mission in conformity with his own principles. In accordance with this arrangement, as long as Ringeltaube resided in Tinnevelly, Kohlhoff paid the salaries of the mission agents through him.

Ringeltaube's letter shows, however, that his view of the situation was rather different from that of Kohlhoff. Regarding the Tinnevelly mission as abandoned by the S.P.C.K., he thought it quite natural to: propose to the London Missionary Society that they should take over the whole mission; and he does not appear to have communicated this proposal to Kohlhoff, or even to have considered the possibility that the S.P.C.K. might not wish to retire from its work in Tinnevelly.

In fact, when in 1807 the authorities of the S.P.C.K. became aware of the arrangement made with Ringeltaube, they objected to it. Rottler defended the action which had been taken at Tanjore, but the Society resolved as follows on February. 4th 1808:

"Agreed in opinion that Missionaries from the Society be informed by the Secretary, that none of the Missionaries from the Anabaptists, and the London Missionary Society, be permitted, on any occasion, to preach or officiate in any of .. The Congregations connected with the Society; - and that no conferences, on Missionary concerns, be ever held with any of them, by the Missionaries connected with this Society."

In the mean time, however, Ringeltaube had worked for nearly two years in Tinnevelly. He was not able to leave Tranquebar till the beginning of February 1806, when, for fear of losing the monsoon, he hired a boat at the expense of forty pagodas to carry him down to Tuticorin, where he landed on the 9th of February. He writes in his journal:

"Going on shore to Tuticorin I introduced myself everywhere as a Missionary, and attended the Dutch Church, a spacious ootagon building, where my countryman the Reverend Mr Cleaver read a good discourse in Dutch to a few attentive hearers. After the sermon; the Tamil Catechist Ráyappan preached to a small congregation of Tamilers and Portuguese. After the close, I addressed them in a few stammering words inviting them in the afternoon to the old fort. At the appointed time I met them to the number of forty or fifty, spake with them individually, and then addressed them (for the first time extempore in Tamil) on the words of St Paul, "'The Spirit bearest witness with our spirit that we are the children of God", I thought I observed soine impression A Portuguese man and woman seemed to be the subjects of saving grace.

"When in the evening sitting in the verandah of the old fort (formerly the abode of power and luxury, now the refuge of a houseless traveller and thousands of bats suspended from the ceiling), enjoying the extensive prospects, and communing with my own heart and the God to whom mercies and forgiveness belong, something frightened me by falling suddenly at my feet and croaking, Parabaran Istotiram, i.e. God be praised (the usual words our Christians pronounced when greeting any one). I rejoiced to see an individual of that tribe among whom I had been so anxious to labour entered into conversation with him, as well as I could, to ascertain his ideas about religion, but was soon nonplussed by his stupidity. I could not force a word from him in answer to my plain questions, which he contented himself with literally giving back to me: With a sigh I was foróed to dismiss him."

On the 11ᵗʰ and 12ᵗʰ he journeyed to Palamcottah, where he stayed till the 17ᵗʰ, and then set out on a tour. He halted at Parpanádapuram, which had two small mud churches, one Roman and the other protestant, and where the catechist Santiago appeared to him to be an honest man but rather ignorant; and in the afternoon proceeded as far as Nazareth, of which he says:

"This is a small place belonging to the Mission. It has a neat clay church - the roof of palmyra leaves... The congregation made a pleasing impression on me."

He slept in the church, and on the next day:

"18ᵗʰ - After having prayed, spoken, and baptized some children, crossed the red hills, an awful desert, formed by the drift: sand blowing from the mountains. If tradition is to be credited, a large town is buried under it. From the top of this elevated plain, you have an enchanting prospect of the sea, Tuticorin, Manappad, Trichendúr, and Palamcottah. The heat was intense, yet I was obliged to walk on foot to ease my little horse. At length we reached a well under some banian trees; rested a little; and proceeded to Jerusalem, another Mission village in a fertile soil. Here we found only a palmyra shed instead of, a church. In the evening passed a little congregation, Nálándula, where the people came to meet me, but I pushed on in order to reach Kulasegarapatnam, near the sea shore. We passed bad clay grounds, where I was obliged to alight, and at nine at night reached our place, where we prayed, and I spoke on the words, 'Abide with us, for the day is far spent!. A good wooden church with an altar. An able man of low caste, Rayappan, is catechist here, and his wife Lydia helps him. He sings well, which is an uncommon talent in India. Slept again in the church at the foot of the altar... About 300 people desire to be baptized; but they do not know why."

"19ᵗʰ - After Morning Prayer, rode along the beach to Manappad, where my friend Mr. Gratian received me cordially, It was he, you know, who encouraged me to come to these parts. Here too is a Dutch factory and a very large church built of stone. In the afternoon spake on the words, Woman! thy sins are forgiven thee,' and baptized eight children. Many people are waiting here for baptism, but they are so ignorant, that I cannot yet make up my mind to grant it; none can give a reason why they wish to be baptized. For the good of my soul', the best instructed of them say, but there the catechization must end, or they are mute. In the dusk, I visited a famous grotto close to the rocky shore under a finë Roman church (there are three in this place) built far out on a projecting point. In this grotto formerly a heathen hermit dwelt, a great saint, and the well that runs in it is still resorted to from superstitious motives"

On the afternoon of the 20th he went on to Attikadu where he prayed in the church, and then:

"Proceeded to Mudalár, not far from it, where there is. A fine stone church and a congregation of 800 souls. This is Mission ground too. The congregation met me rejoicing, the poor creatures thinking that a Missionary must bring them golden times. Before the church stands a building like a pigeon-house with a large kettle-drum to convoke the congregation. Its sound is heard deep into the palmyra woods. Honest young Abraham from Tanjore presides over this flock; there is a good school in this village. I spoke this evening upon the first commandment. The boys answered very sensibly. Afterwards Maduranayagam, a catechist from Tanjore, requested that he might address the people. I granted this request of course, and was astonished at his gifts. He catechized on the parable of the prodigal with uncommon fluency Service being ended, the people flocked to me to speak, of their souls? Ah no! of their petty quarrels and complaints. How much was I discouraged by this scene from going on with my work."

Early on the 21st he walked back to Attikadu to baptize a child, and then returned to Mudalur. Here

"Complaints poured so thick upon me that at eleven o'clock I rode off, notwithstanding the heat being tremendous.I certainly was too impatients, but I am but a young beginner. After an hour reached Vijayaramapuran, a young congregation, that had just built a palmyra shed for a church. Here I prayed, feeling still indisposed to preach from the scene that had passed, and rode slowly on to another village."

At noon he rested at Sáttánkulam, and in the evening proceeded to Periyakulam,

"Wherewallittle congregation, "about fifteen in number, have built a palmyra church. They were formerly Roman Catholics, and left their church owing to a quarrel with the priest. The congregation at this place is in a state of great ignorance.it

He returned to Palamcottah the next day, and stayed there till March 3rd; he then started on another tour, in which, after visiting Parpanadapuram and Periyakulam, and sleeping a second night at sattankulam, he went on towards the villages in the south-west.

"5th - Struck off into a new path more to the southward, and breakfasted at a place called Bethany, where there is a handsome church, and a considerable village belonging to the Mission; here, I convened the people and chose and blessed elders, to whom I committed my instructions, by way of trial, and prayed, and spoke agreeably to the occasion. After breakfast went to Ilaikulam, a small village in the woods, where three months ago the people turned their pagodas into a Christian church. They were all abroad, and I therefore passed on to Vemmanangudi, where I addressed the congregation on the words, Our Father, which art in heaven. ? The people here shewed great affection to me, and ran me half a mile, with a vessel full of palmyra juice fresh drawn from the tree."

"About sunset I arrived at Uyari, a charming village close to the sea, with three Roman Catholic Churches. Proofs of industry beyond what is generally met with in this country appeared everywhere. The people have taken considerable pains to cultivate a narrow strip of sand running parallel with the shore, Luxuriant tobacco plantations, with plaintain and cucumber gardens, salute the eye wearied out by the red desert. Here I thought I should like to fix my abode. . I preached in the evening, and on the following day settled many disagreeable affairs by di smissing a catechist who had long been very obnoxious. This is the same man who is known in Europe as a chief of the Shanars that embraced and preached the Gospel. Five hundred neophytes fell away in a late persecution (as it is called), but all the baptized people remained steadfast to the number of two hundred."

"6th - In the evening proceeded to Kundal, a Christian village on the shore, with a handsome church, some miles from Uvari. Preached and baptized several children. After sermon a man came and told me of his own accord that he was a great sinner, and wished to have somebody sent to him to instruct him. I rejoiced to hear for the first time a spontaneous declaration of this kind from an Indian, and pointed out to: him our All-sufficient Saviour. His name is Oliyu, i.e., splendour. I wish I may hereafter have an opportunity to give a good account of him."

"8th - Went out to Marakundal(2), another Christian village on the shore, where I preached, baptized some children, and requested Mengnanam, a worthy catechist from Tanjore, to take care of the congregation at Uvari ad interim. There are some promising young men at this place, who might easily be trained for teachers.'"

"I proceeded from hence to Navaladi, another Christian village of the same description. Daniel a steady young man from the Tanjore Seminary is here, as well as many fine boys that can read and write. Nothing would be more easy than to form a Seminary in this country. In the evening I proceeded inland to podúr, but did not like the aspect of the congregation."

He returned to Palamcottah and stayed there till after Easter, and then set off on the 13th of April for Travancore, spending eleven days in visiting again the stations in the south. He particularly mentions Samariapuram, and Vadakkankulam, where he found about thirty Protestants, but many Catholics, who were hostile On the 25th he crossed over into Travancore, where he visited various places, and stayed there for two and a half months, reaching Palamcottah again on the 10th July. Between them and September he made five more tours in south Tinnevelly, of which, however, he gives no details. Of Palamcottah itself he remarks that the English service there was in general attended by twenty to forty-five people, and the Tamil congregation amounted to the same number.

Ringeltaube closes this section of his journal with general remarks on the state of the congregations. His judgements are clearly those of a man of deep and enthusiastic piety, and his expectations somewhat high-pitched. It must be remembered that at this time he had little knowledge of Tamil, at any rate as spoken in the villages, and cannot therefore have gained very close contact with the catechists and congregations whom he met. He says in his journal:

"Being as yet unable to understand the dialect of this province, and having no means whatever to distinguish proper subjects for baptism, I gave the power of baptizing (as is : sometimes done) to two worthy catechists, Mangnanam and Abraham, and between three and four hundred adults have been, baptized (3)."

Some of his remarks may be quoted:

"On the principle that whosoever professes to believe in Jesus as God and Saviour is to be baptized, this Mission has hitherto been conducted. In general, however, it is. expected of the candidates for baptism, that they should know by heart the Creed, the Lord's prayer, and the words implying the institution of the two Sacraments by Christ, and that the children, at least, born in the congregation, should know by heart the Creed, the Lord's prayer, and the words implying the institution of the two Sacraments by Christ, and that the children, at least, born in the congregation, should know these thoroughly. Thus we have a little wheat mixed with a great proportion of tares, as in other places; yet I have some times, though but seldom, heard short and feeling prayers, and caught occasionally a sigh. that came from the heart. Upon inquiry, I find that out of many professors, there are but few that walk under the influence of the Gospel; yet I firmly believe that the doctrine of salvation.becomes more and more lively in the hearts of those who might at first, have embraced it from unworthy motives, especially at the approach of that admirable preacher Death and did not the Lord's Apostles themselves follow him; at first, from selfish motives, having worldly grandeur and personal profit in view? Yet the Lord did not forbid them to be baptized on this account, but bore with them. for a good and great purpose."

"The tribe of Shánars is very numerous both here and in Travancore. In the latter country, I do not know if they resemble in all respects our Shánars. In this district I compute them to be at least fifty congregations, under the care of about thirty native teachers. A few of the latter (perhaps eight or ten) are rather respectable servants of God, as far as their knowledge goes. But the greater, parts have been enlisted in a hurry from among. The Shanars themselves, reading and writing being the only .quality required. From these catechists, and their deceitful and unworthy conduct, my worst troubles arise. But till a Seminary for forming better ones is established in these parts, the evil must be borne with, and the only thing I can do is to keep them in awe. It is also to be lamented that many of them receive too little wages. If they have families, they can scarcely afford to buy a little palmyra sugar to satisfy the cravings of nature. My heart bleeds for them in this respect, for this. Extreme poverty often prompts them' to take bribes and presents to do what they should not."

"Persecution, in the proper sense of the word, has not occurred since my arrival. Those oppressions and extortions before mentioned, when befalling Christians, have been represented as persecution; but it is certain that the heathens, Mahometans and Roman Catholics suffer more by them than our Christians, So much so, that sometimes the former offer money, and use other means, to obtain the protection of the Missionary. But all these, it is reported, will soon be done away by a fixed rate of taxes."

He ends by putting the following plan before the London Missionary Society:

"I consider myself bound in conscience to decline taking any part of the established Mission into my hands; our brethren at home, not hearing any account of a work of God in the hearts of the converts, would soon be discouraged. I would by no means have this interpreted as a disparagement of the existing Mission. I hope in one shape or other God's own finger will appear.

"My plan is as follows:

1. A small congregation to be begun near the confines of Travancore; £100 to be devoted to buying ground and erecting necessary buildings.

2. A close communion to be established among real converts, by means of a frequent enjoyment of the Lord's Supper granted only to such.

These are the outlines of my plan. Its expense would. not exceed £200 per annum. Á more effectual one I cannot devise. It would, among other advantages, throw into our hands some youths, who after a little preparation may be usefully employed in establishing Christianity almost independently, if European Missionaries cannot soon be found. Should this old Mission be long without en European to keep it in order, it may rapidly increase in numbers, but will certainly lose the grand essentials of a Christian Church, for which we all should be heartily Sorry,"

A letter of almost the same date to Mr. Robert Cowie of the London Missionary Society gives further details of his plans for the seminary, for which, he says, he has already two Christian boys in training:

"A Seminary of twelve youths to be erected and maintained. The annual expense of a boy, 18 star pagodas; total 216 star

er annum, equal to £82. These youths, when fit, to be employed as itinerants; and every one so employed to receive two star pagodas per month."

Ringeltaube's journal from October 1806 to August 180'7 shows that at the end of October he received letters from a friend at Anjengo, who sent him 100 star pagodas, and, gave him hopes of being able to buy, a suitable site at Mayiladi, a few miles, across the Travancore-Tinnevelly border. This decided him to carry out the general plan, he had put before the London Missionary Society, and in December he went up to Trichinopoly to discuss the matter with the S.P.C.K. missionaries. One infers that they persuaded him to continue some supervision of the congregations in south Tinnevelly, since for the next eight months he gave a good deal of attention to them, while seeking for a place to settle in which would be convenient for both Tinnevelly and Travancore. : In February he bought a field close to Canaanúr(4), just on the Tinnevelly side of the border, and began a 'singing schooli there, but from May to August he was staying at Mudalúr, and while there, bought a plot of ground at Taruvai, built a small bungalow, and in August was intending to settle there. Some extracts from the journal may be given.

"Oct. 21st - Stopped at a little church (near Padukapattu, built a few days ago, the people rejoiced to see me, and desired leave to call their settlement after my name, but I called it Nain and spoke on the nature of true fa th. From thence rode-to Sundakottai, where there is also a new church or rather palmyra shed."

"Oct. 25 th - Rode to Ilankulam. Their pagoda is now turned into a good little church, and they have a catechist. Preceded to Taruvai, prayed in a new shed, where they are going to build a church."

"Mar. 1st 1807 - Began a singing school with the children of Canaanúr, where I expect to be able to settle. What a hopeless task this is, none of our brethren in Europe can conceive. All these little creatures sing a gruff bass, and for their life cannot command more than three notes in the scale,"

"Aug. 13th - (On hearing a man praying at night in the fields) - I hope there is a little spiritual life among these people and more there would appear probably, were the Missionary more spiritually affected. I must confess I like them a great deal better since I have lived among them."

"Aug. 23rd. My progress in the Tamil language is such as enables me to discourse on religious subjects so as to be. Understood. Elegance, fluency, and eloquence I have not yet obtained. Moreover, I find it very difficult to understand the natives, partly from their speaking incorrectly, uncouthly, provincially, and partly from the rapidity of their elocution."

He expresses the wish that the British and Foreign Bible Society might give a grant for the purchase of Tamil Bibles, which would do more than all the catechists together; and ends this journal with the words

My wish is to try at Taruvai, where I may do as I:: please, to raise a small flock of Christians, that have something of the powers of the world to come in their soul's; I mean love, which endureth for ever.!!

No journal's or letters from Ringeltaube for 1808 seem to have survived, and at the end of that year, or early in 1809, his direct connexion with Tinnevelly came to an end. Bishop Caldwell states that he handed over to the representatives of the S.P.C.K. the bungalow be had built at Taruvai and also the piece of ground on which Canaanúr stood. From 1808 to 1816 he continued to work in Travancore, residing for a time at Oodagherry but chiefly at Mayiladi. During these years he . Gathered congregations in some seven villages, which in 1815 included about 840 baptized persons, and had schools in about five villages. One of these villages, Pichaikudiyiruppu, was just on the English side of the Travancore border; the others were all in south Travancore.

He visited Palamcottah several times, and spent Christmas there at least twice, taking services for the English and perhaps also for the Tamil congregation there. He kept up a warm friendship with Mr. Sawyer till the latter's death in 1815, (5) and in the previous year had proposed that Mr Sawyer should join him, not (as he had suggested in 1805) merely as an assistant, but as a full Missionary. Mr. Sawyer was willing, but the plan was not approved by the British Resident in Travancore, who suggested instead that Rhenius or Schnarré, who had just then arrived at Tranquebar under the C.M.S., might come to work in South Travancore. Ringeltaube, however, did not think that it would be wise for missionaries of two different societies to attempt to work together, and decided to resign in favour of the C.M.S. missionaries, though, just as when he first came to Tinnevelly himself, he does not seem to have considered what the wishes of his own society might be in such a matter. But Rhenius, fearing to embroil the societies, declined the proposal.

At the beginning of 1816, feeling weak and worn, and suffering from liver disease, Ringeltaube left Travancore. In announcing his departure to the Directors of the London Missionary Society he wrote that, f'My work is done and finished, so as to bear the stamp of permanencyil, and since the Society had for the last two years been endeavouring to find him a colleague, he doubtless hoped (as proved to be the case) that, his congregations would not be left uneared for. He intended to take a voyage to the Cape of Good Hope to recuperate his health, but for reasons of which we have no information went instead to Malacca, and wrote from there to the Treasurer of the L.M.S. and to his sister, saying that his health was slightly better, and that he was going on to Batavia, and had some idea of endeavouring to do missionary work on the west coast of Sumatra. No more was ever heard of him, and it seems most probable that he died on the voyage,

Ringeltaube's work in Tinnevelly was short, but his memory has lasted there as well as in his main field of work, South Travancore. Except in the important point that he did not value poverty or asceticism as of direct spiritual value, he may fairly be described as the earliest Protestant missionary sadhu. A small hut to live in and village food to eat were sufficient for his needs, he seldom had a coat to his back except when furnished with one by Col. Trotter of Palamcottah or some other friend, and he. spent his salary on the poor of his congregations. Such a life, led by a man of deep personal devotion to his Saviour, who visibly lived in and by the spirit of prayer, was appreciated and admired by Indians. Englishmen, however, while acknowledging his earnestness and devotion, regarded him rather as an eccentric, Mr. Hough in his History of Christianity in India (Vol. IV, p.284, quoted in Caldwel. I, p.1661.) gives a distinctly depreciatory view of his character, and it must be acknowledged that he probably represents accurately the views of missionaries and others who had known Ringeltaube well. He was certainly erratic in his plans of action, and, as his journals and correspondence with the L.M.S. show, was capable of putting forward, apparently in all seriousness, ideas and schemes which can only be called extraordinary.

For the years 1808 to 1816 we have only very scanty accounts of the missionary work in Tinnevelly. This is partly due to the almost complete failure of our main sources of information - the reports and letters of the Tanjore and Trichinopoly missionaries which were published in the Neuere Geschichte, from which we have so often quoted in the preceding chapters. The editors of this were able to publish no new parts between 1808 and 1815, and. explain in the latter year that owing to the war in Europe. Very few communications had come through for several years, and that they had not received several diaries and reports which the missionaries were known to have sent off. A few diaries and letters of the period were, however, ultimately published in the Neuere Geschichte, and some communications from the missionaries are to be found in the S.P.C.K. East India Mission Committee's reports. But a larger reason for the lack of information about Tinnevelly is that the missionaries could report so little about the life of the Church there. None :of them visited minnevelly during these years, and Sattiyanadan only made one short visit in 1810; and only for the last two or three years of the period was an Indian priest stationed in the district.

During this period, the "English Missionariesit were. Pohle at Trichinopoly and Kohlhoff at Tanjore. Horst, after working with Gericke for eleven years as a schoolmaster at Vepery, was ordained in 1806, and joined Kohlhoff at Tanjore, but died in 1810. They felt keenly the need of Indian priests, and in 1807 were contemplating the ordination of some catechists, but we are told, (6)

"Deemed it prudent to postpone this, till a more favourable period should arrive, when a more regular. Church Establishment should be instituted, which the Indian religious public and the Missionaries so much wished for, and under which ordinations might be performed with more authority and regularity."

This hope for the creation of an Anglican episcopate in India, however, was premature, and the S.P.C.K. in 1810 asked their whether Syrian priests could not be employed in the South India Missions. Kohlhoff and Horst replied with a memorandum in which they stated that they felt bound to decline a union with those priests, since they held doctrines which militated against the Thirty-nine Articles, the Augustan Confession, and the Nicene Creed.: Pohle concurred, but suggested that the present situation of the Syrians might come to be better known if some person acquainted with their language were to reside among them for a year or two.

Finally the missionaries determined that they could wait no longer, and, the S.P.C.K. Offering no objections, Pohle, Kohlhoff and Sattiyanadan ordained four catechists at Trichinopoly on the 17th March, 1811, - Gnánapragasan, Adaikalam, Vedanayagam and Abraham - and Vedanayagam was immediately sent to Palamcottah to take charge of the Tinnevelly congregations.

His work there, however, was short, since he died at Palamcottah in 1813 of the fever that was then raging. Abraham was sent to replace him, but he also was taken seriously ill and had to return to Tanjore, and could not go to Tinnevelly again before 1815 or 1816.

A very severe epidemic of fever, in fact, swept over the Tinnevelly, Madura, and Rámnád districts from 1811 end of 1810 there was heavy rain and very seyere floods, and in the following February rain fell again very heavily for ten days, and there were further large falls of rain in March and April, a most unusual season for anything more than a few light showers or slight thunderstorms. This caused an epidemic. of fever, probably a specially severe form of malaria, to spread from the western hills outwards into the whole district. The fever was of an extremely virulent type, many, who were attacked by it dying within three days. The mortality was terrible; in some places half the population were said to have died, and the loss of labour combined with the effects of the floods soon brought about famine conditions. It is stated that in the town of Ramnad one in six died during the three months from December 1812 to February 1813, and Pohle reported that in consequence of the famine, thousands of people had fled from the southern districts to the neighbourhood of Trichinopoly. A medical committee was convened by the authorities in May of 1811, but most of their recommendations, such as that the people should sleep on cots, should clothe themselves more warmly, and should eat better food, were not likely to be of much practical value to villagers who were already half starving through loss of crops.

Vedanayagam wrote to Kohlhoff in August 1811. that already more than 20,000 had died of the pestilential fever in the Tinnevelly district, and that the fever, combined with certain additional taxes which the inhabitants of all other districts of the Tinnevelly province were exempted from, had obliged almost all the Christians in his districtx to disperse into different places and to settle in other villages of heathen, Partly by the numbers who had been carried off by the fever and partly by the falling off(**X 1.e., the Karaisuttu or southern coast district.**)of many, the Christian body in Tinnevelly had suffered a great diminution.

A letter of the missionaries in 1812 says that they could report nothing about Dindigul or Madura owing to the fever. It had affected people's morals seriously, and Christians,. Unhappily, had given a bad example to others. In 1813 they again reported that the fever had continued to rage in those districts and that they could not send any .catechist there; by the beginning of 1814, however, they were able to write that people had again begun to settle at Dindigul and Madura, and that since small garrisons had also been stationed at those places, they hoped that there would before long be Christians of the Mission living there. This, in fact, soon happened, and at the end of 1815 there were fifty-two Christians at Madura and Dindigul. Kohlhoff wrote in 1814 that. the small congregation at Sivaganga had lately received a considerable increase, and he wished to erect a chapel there, but could not get a piece of ground (7).

In 1816, Bishop Middleton, who had arrived at Calcutta in: November 1814 as the first. Bishop of Calcutta, passed through Tinnevelly on his way to Cochin, and had a fleeting glimpse cf the

Palamcottah congregation. In a letter dated the 22nd March, 1816, he writes:

"You will observe that I date from Palamcottah, the capital of Tinnevelly in the south of India. Cape Comorin, its southern extremity - (or rather, the immense mountain which though twenty miles from the sea is the marinersi land-mark and is falsely called the Cape) - raises its lofty projecting head full in view from the window at which I am now writing, at the distance of only forty miles. In a few days I am to pass very near it, on my way to Travancore, and at Cochin (whither, as the papers inform me, a ship has Bombay to convey the Bishop to that Presidency), I am once more to commit myself to the ocean."

"I have on the course of my journey met with hardly anything more interesting than the scene of yesterday evening. I was encamped a few miles from this place (for we are dwellers in tents, and frequently do not see anything better than a few native huts for many days together), when, after rising from dinner, I was informed that several persons were in waiting to pay their respects. I went out and received, as is usual at every stage, the compliments of the Darogah, a sort of chief constable of the hundred, with all his followers, who prigested fruit, eto, When I had dismissed them, another party came up, for whom I was not so well prepared. It was a deputation of thirty or forty Brahmans, from the Tinnevelly Pagodas, who also came to pay their respects to the Bishop and represent that the Government allowed them so little out of the produce of their lands, that they and their religion were in danger of being starved; and they looked to me, very naturally to be sure, to interfere in their behalf! To understand this you must be told that the Government are here a sort of lay-impropriators. They take the Pagoda estates into their own hands, and grant out of the proceeds what they think reasonable for the performance of the duty and the expense of the ceremonies; and in this instance the Brahmans say it is not onough. The question is entirely out of my cognizance; but the Company's servants very generally assure me that the allowances of Government for such purposes are extremely liberal."

"But the delightful part is yet to come. I have with me a writer, David, who joined me at Tanjore (the son of Sattiyanadan, whose sermon you have at the Society), and he informed me that the party who stood aloof were Christians who came from Palancottah, to welcome me and to receive my blessing. I went forward to meet them. They were headed by their native priest and my man David. They were about thirty, and they formed the most remote congregation under Mr Kohlhoff's care. The priest, a very interesting man, whose countenance, if I recollect rightly, resembles the head of St Cyprian in Cave's Lives (but the book is at Calcutta, 1200 miles off), and has almost the darkest complexion I have seen, addressed me on behalf of his people; and in reply I gave them a suitable exhortation, which David interpreted with great energy, and they received it with every mark of thankfulness. They then opened their Tamil Prayer-books, and sang a Psalm of thanksgiving to a tune, which I dare say is used at Hackney, quite correctly and in good tune and melody. The Brahmans witnessed the scene and both deputations: quitted the camp together,"

The Bishop had received these deputations at his last camp before reaching Palamcottah; we hear through a letter of Col. Trotter's to Pohle that he also saw something of the Mission in Palamcottah itself. On the Saturday, the day after the Bishop had written the letter quoted above, he breakfasted with Col. Trotter, and after breakfast,

"I took him to the church, where at the entrance of the churchyard the Country Priests. Catechists, and ali, the Christians were drawn out in two lines singing a hymn - the schoolboys were all sitting down on the ground with their : cajan books - he visited the little church, looked all over it, and asked many questions. I showed him the Mission Ground where a house now fallen down once stood, and garden. I desired the school boys to write on the sand to show him our Indian method, at which he seemed much pleased, to see the Madras system so well exemplified, because he mentioned the disputes between Mr. Lancaster and Dr. Bell, and he appears to be on the side of the latter - he was very curious and asked many questions"

The Bishop stayed, at Palamcottah over the Sunday, and divine service was held at his quarters. (8)

NOTES AND REFERENCES - CHAPTER VI

1) Ringeltaube was born in 1770 at Schiedelwitz in Silesia, and i educated at Halle; he was ordained in 1796 at Wernigerode, and was at Calcutta as a missionar of the S.P.C.K. from 1797 to 1799.

For a general account of his life, see Ringeltaube the Rishi, by W. Robinson, Sheffield 1902, C.L.S. Madras 1908. For fuller details, and for his journals, see Minutes of the Proceedings of the Directors of the (London) Missionary Society, and Transactions of the Missionary Society. Caldwell gives considerable extracts from the Transactions, and also the detailed story of Vedamánikkam, as told by a rela the Madras Tract Society's Tamil Magazine in 1841.

2) Query, the same as Marakáttuvilai, no. 25 in Sattiyanádan's list given in Appendix A.

3) A baptism register preserved in the S.P.G. office, Tanjore,shows that the places of baptism included Attikádu Kúdankulan (42), Vadakkankulam (36), Ilaikulam (1 Bethaniyapuram (71), Anaikulam (110), and Jerusalem (45).

4) "Canaanúr" is the same as South Kannankulam, a village close to the sea coast about a quarter of a mile from the Travancore border. A plot of land of about four acres adjoining the village is even now called Mission-Vilaill, and is presumably the land bought by Ringeltaube. Part of it has now become house-plots, and the remainder was in 1938 still in the possession of the L.M.S.

Local tradition states that one Sivamurthi, the son of a Roman Catholic from Sivakasi who, after marrying a Hindu woman, had lapsed from Christianity and had come to live at Kannankulam, came to Ringeltaube in Palamcottah, received instruction from him, and was baptized (with the name of Jebamurthi) with his five children in 1809. This is said to have been the first Christian family in the village, and Jebamurthi's son Swaminádan to have been the first catechist in the village.

Ringeltaube may have continued to visit Canaanur after his leaving Tinnevelly, but he never mentions it in his journal after 1809.

5) Mr. Sawyer died on Nov. 18th, 1815, and his tomb is to be seen in the old Burial Ground, Palamcottah. His chief memorial. Is, of course, the village of Sawyerpuram, the land of which he bought in 1810 for the formation of a Christian village.

6. For the correspondence of the missionaries with the S.P.C.K., the ordination in 1811, etc., see Pohle's journal for 1811 in Neuere Geschichte, Bd, VI, St. 70, and S.P.C.K., East India Mission Committee, Vol. S. 61.

Dr. (then Mr.) Claudius Buchanan, then Vice-Provost of the College of Fort William at Calcutta, published in 1805 a Memoir of the Expediency of an Ecclesiastical Establishment for British India, which excited general attention in England, and the scheme was heartily approved by the Archbishop of Canterbury, and other English bishops, though opposition was raised in certain quarters. On his return to England in 1808, Dr. Buchanan pressed forward the scheme and developed it in detail, proposing four dioceses of Bengal, Madras, Bombay, and Ceylon with Java and other eastern islands in the possession of Great Britain. The Government accepted the general principle, and an Act was passed in 1813, which provided, however, for only one bishopric, with three archdeacons. See Buchanan's Memoirs.

7) For further details of the epidemic, see Caldwell, pp.170 ff., an Appendix in Bishop Caldwell's History of Tinnevelly, and the Tinnevelly District Gazetteer. The epidemic seems to have been very similar to that which raged in central and northern Ceylon in 1935. Malaria is endemic in Tinnevelly only on the edge of the western hills.

For the correspondence referred to, see the box "C. India'l in the S.P.G. archives, the S.P.C.K. minutes, and the Neuere Geschichte, Bd. VI, st. 66 and 70.

8) Life of Bishop Middleton, by C.W. Le Bas; and for Col. Trotteris letter see the box "C. India" in the S.P.G. archives.

THE REBUILDING OF THE TINNEVELLY CHURCH – HOUGH, 1816 to 1821; THE BEGINNINGS OF C.M.S. WORK IN TINNEVELLY UNDER RHENIUS AND SCHMID,1820 to 1823

Only a few months after Bishop Middleton's passing visit, there arrived in Palamcottah the man who may-rightly be called the second founder of the Church in Tinnevelly, who began to revivify the work of the S.P.C.K., and was the means of the C.M.S. beginning their long and magnificent services to the Tinnevelly Church - the Rev. James Hough.

Mr. Hough was born in 1789 and ordained in 1814. For some years before his ordination, he had wished to give himself to missionary work, and in 1815 he met the great. Evangelical leader Charles Simeon, who was seeking for keen young Evangelical clergymen to go out to India as chaplains, and through him received his appointment as a chaplain under the Company. He arrived at Madras in August 1816, was appointed to Pälamcottah as Military Chaplain, and reached the station on November 2nd, being welcomed by the good friend of the Mission, Col. Trotter the Commandant.(1)

He immediately began to develop missionary schools in connexion with the Church Missionary Society, which by this time had been working for several years in South India. The Society had begun by giving grants to aid the schools of the Tranquebar Mission in 1812, when that Mission was in serious' straits owing to the help from Denmark having been cut off when Tranquebar was surrendered to the English in 1810, moreover, of the two then remaining missionaries, Rev. A.F. Caemmerer the elder and Dr. John, the latter was very old and infirm. In 1814 the C.M.S. enlarged their help, and directly began work in South India by sending out Rhenius and Schnarre to Tranquebar, and in November of that year a Corresponding Committee of the Society was formed in Madras. A Missionary Association in connexion with the C.M.S. was formed, among the members of which were chaplains who were ready, as far as their primary duties should permit, a to engage actively in promoting the views of the Societyis; and the First Annual Report of the Madras Corresponding Committee, published in 1818, includes under the heading of Chaplains Stations' reports from the chaplains of Masulipatam, Vellore, Chittoo, Tellicherry, and Palamcottah (2).

Mr. Hough had only been two months in Palancottah when he opened an English school there, which was attended by children of the public servants and of the native officers of the battalion, and also a Tamil school in the Fort and in July of 1817 he. Opened another Tamil school at Palamcottah. For these schools he erected two schoolrooms at his own expense, sent an Indian teacher to Tranquebar for training, engaged an English schoolmaster, and later in the year added to his establishment another Indian teacher, who had formerly been supported by Mr. Sawyer. In. September of 1817, the three schools had a total number of 169 pupils. His first attempts to persuade the English residents of Palamcottah to subscribe to help this work among the Hindus and Christians were not at all successful, but, as he writes,

"At length the Collector, John Cotton Esq. receiving an application for contributions to a school at Cochin, considered that if inclined 'to support such institutions, they ought to : begin with those of their own chaplain. In consequence he. Requested to be informed of what had been done, and contributed. Liberally towards the expenses incurred. His example was followed by his neighbours; and from this time they subscribed annually to the maintenance of the schools."

During 1817, in fact, Rs.800 were subscribed at Palamcottah.

In June of 1818, Mr. Hough, on the request of many parents, opened a second English school in Tinnevelly and in July and December Tamil schools at lachanallúr and. Mélapalaiyan. In the two English schools the New Testament, the Psalter, and Sellonis History of the Bible were used. He also at the beginning of the year opened a school at Tuticorin, but owing to the opposition of the Roman Catholics to the appointment of a Protestant schoolmaster, he finally had to appoint á Hindu master, and the school did not succeed, and was closed after about a year. The Madras Corresponding Committee made a grant for the school work of twenty pagodas monthly, and sanctioned the purchase of a ground and building in Tinnevelly for 300 pagodas. At the end of the year, Mr. Hough made another important beginning by opening a Seminary, or as we should now call it, a Boarding School at.. Palamcottah for the Christian boys with a view to providing future. Catechists. Village work also began in this year by his sending a catechist to Sidambarapuram and Kannankulam, whence a request for teaching had come.

It does not seem that Mr. Hough had got into any effective touch with the S.P.C.K. village congregations before the summer of 1818, but his attention was then called to them by a request from the Madras District Committee of the S.P.C.K. for a report on the work of that Society in the district. This Committee had been formed in 1815 with the objects of inviting subscriptions to the Society and extending the use of its publications. Its responsibilities were, however, soon enlarged, for on the death in November 1817 of p'ázold, the senior S.P.C.K. missionary at Madras, the Committee, on the request of Pohle and Kohlhoff, took chatge of the mission at Madras, and on Pohle's death at Trichinopoly only two months later, it assumed supervisory charge of the whole of the S.P.C.K. missionary work in South India. It at once asked for reports from Kohlhoff at Tanjore, and from the chaplains at Cuddalore, Trichinopoly, and Palamcottah, on the present state of the missionary work at those stations, and Hough replied on the 10 th September 1818 with a careful and fairly long report. It is from this report, and from the further reports which he sent in September 1819, August 1820 and March 1821, that we can gain most of our information on the state of the Tinnevelly congregations when he came to the district, and on what he himself did to strengthen the work. (3)

Abraham, apparently posted at Palamcottah, was in 1818. still the only Indian minister in the district,, but pohle had in 1817 ordained three more catechists, Pakkiyanadan, Nallatambi, and, Visuvasanádan (also called Abraham), and the last-named was sent in 1819 to join Abraham in Tinnevelly, and was stationed at Nazareth, Abraham at the same time going to Mudalúr: Hough thought well of Visuvasanadan and in his report of 1819 wrote of: him,

"He seems to be a man of respectable abilities and genuine piety, and the discourse I heard him preach to his own congregation would have done credit to a minister possessed of the advantage of a superior education to that which he has received."

After he had left Tinnevelly, he wrote of him in 1824,

"His piety, ability, and Christian meekness commanded the love of the Native Converts, and the respect of the Heathen and Mahomedans."

He notes that Abraham's salary at this time (and presumably Visuvasanádan's also) was about seven star pagodas per mensem.si

The catechists' salaries and the travelling charges of Abraham amounted to about thirty-five star pagodas monthly, this being paid out of the interest on the fund left by Schwartz.(4)

Presumably on information given him by Abraham, Hough reported in 1818 that there were altogether sixty-three congregations, large and small, with a total Christian population of 2830; there were also 270 Christians of the Tinnevelly establishment in the neighbouring villages of Travancore. Some of the congregations numbered upwards of 400.

"Of these Christians some are respectable inhabitants, such as farmers, and others of that class; but they appear to consist chiefly of mechanics as of the Toddy Cast: I have not yet seen a Pariar among them and I believe there are very few. 11

It would appear from Hough is last remark that he had not yet come to know of the congregations at Parpanadapuram and Púváni.

The baptisms for the year 1814 to 1818 were as follows:
Children 1814 1815 1816 1817 1818 Total
Heathen converts 46 162 106 98 117 529
<u>Roman Catholic converts 4 13 5 13 0 35 </u>
Totals 62 236 180 136 169 783
The communicants in 181 were 127: the deaths from 1814 to 1818 inclusive were 147.

It seems that Hough had been able to visit some of the village centres before making his first report, and he could not write at all favourably either of the schools or of the general level of the congregational life.

"The schools are in a very indifferent state, as there are no schoolmasters on the establishment, they are entrusted to the care of the catechists, who, from some cause or other, are seldom found attentive to their charge. The system of education adopted does not appear to differ from the common country mode of teaching; very few of the schools possess a single book, they are, consequently, obliged to use such cadjan X writings and stories as they can get; and I need not remark to the Committee of what sad materials, in a moral point of view, these are ordinarily composed. óó..The schools are in a deplorable state, and hence the almost heathen darkness of the majority of the people, numbers scarcely know why they are Christians, and the first principles of their religion are novel Sounds to their ears. No wonder, therefore, that their conduct should be calculated to disgust their heathen neighbours rather than fill them with admiration. They have no light in themselves, it is impossible then that they can 'so shine before men that they may see their good works and glorify their Father which is in heaven."

He therefore urged the Committeee to appoint schoolmasters (whose pay would be but là pagodas per mensem), and also begged (X Palm-leaf)them to send him Tamil books - Testaments, The Pilgrim's Progress, Hymns, Catechisms, etc. Books were sent, and in his report of September 1819 he wrote that they had been eagerly asked for, and that he needed many more. He also described a recent visit to Nazareth and Mudalur:

"If I may judge from appearances during my short stay among the people of these two villages, they are much attached to their Priests as are the Christians of the surrounding country, and I am persuaded they only require to be well supported and encouraged to prove of the most essential service to the congregations entrusted to their care: Even from my hasty visit, the joy diffused through all classes was indescribable, and the people flocked in from the neighbouring vill?ges in every direction. On catechizing such as were introduced to me as the principal people, I found them much better taught in their religion than I had anticipated; and considering the space of time that they have been without a Missionary, it was highly gratifying and encouraging to find the benign and peaceable genius of Christianity still keeping them at unity amongst themselves. The two villages named above, consist entirely of Protestants. One of the priests led me to a part of the village, where was seated under the shade of a cocoanut: tree a considerable company of women spinning cotton and singing I11.theran hymns to the motion of their wheels. After Service a great part of the congregtion shewed no disposition to disperse, and seating themselves round the door, sang their hymns to a late hour.

There were two old men among the group who were converted to the Christian faith by your Missionary.Gericke about twenty years ago, and they sang to me several hymns he had taught them... What they sang or said was not so intelligible, indeed, as the language of younger men, but. You will readily imagine them to have been among the most is interesting of the Company."

"I state these, perhaps, trifling particulars, to shew that there appears to be something more than the bare name of · Christianity here, and that the enemies of Missionary exertions are mistaken in asserting, that there is not a genuine convert to Christianity among the native protestants. No, Sir, if the Society for Promoting Christian Knowledge had no other fruit of their cares, their exertions and their expenditures for the promoting of Christian knowledge' in India to produce they might point triumphantly to these two villages in proof that their labour has not been in vain. I have seldom witnessed so much religion in a town in England as is conspicuous here; and some heathen in the neighbourhood of one of the villages told me candidly that it was a very quiet and good place."

"I spoke, with the priests, of the Tamil Liturgy that you propose sending hither, and recommended them to adopt it. in all the churches in room of the German form of worship now in use; and they readily acceded to the proposition."

During 1819 Mr. Hough had opened on the C.M.S. account Tamil schools at Tinnevelly, Tinnevelly Pettai, Kurichi, Nazareth, and Mudalur, and also started a second seminary at Nazareth; at the end of the year, the Palamcottah seminary had eight pupils, of whom three were about 17 years old, and the others from 12 to 15 years old, under the catechist and sexton of Palamcottah as teacher; the Nazareth Seminary had so far only three pupils, and was taught by Visuvasanadan. Each pupil received a scholarship of half a pagoda monthly.(5)

In 1820, the Madras Committee of the S.P.C.K., with the hearty approbation of the Bishop of Calcutta, made a grant of Rs:40 a' month from May for their school work in Tinnevelly; Mr. Hough therefore arranged with the C.M.S. Corresponding Committee that those of the schools supported by them which were at S.P.C.K. villages (which by then included newly started schools at Kulasegarapatnam and Taruvai, and, after much persuasion of the people, schools for girls at Nazareth and Mudalur should be transferred to the S.P.C.K. account. By the time he made his third report to the S.P.C.K. in August 1820, the transfer had been made, and two more schools at S.P.C.K. villages had been opened, so that the S.P.C.K. schools were as given in the following table:

Station No. of: scholars
Parlamcottah 42
Nazareth. Boys 34
Nazareth. Girls 10
Mudalur boys 47
Mudalur girls 11
Kulasegarapatnam 38
Täruvai 26
Patti 25
Hooprumcottäh 50
Total 283

The last-named place is, probably Hough-ur (later called Hough-aiyyarpuram) or Attikádu, where Hough had settled some · families of poor and scattered Christians, in gratitude for .. which the place was called after his name. It is possible; however, that it represents a mis-reading of Vgramcottah, Thhirankottar.

The C.M.S. schools at the end of 1819 were as follows:
Station No. of pupils.
English
Palamcottah 38
Tinnevelly. 21
Tamil 59
Palamcottah.. 57
Tachanallur. 41
Melapalaiyam' 52

Tinnevelly 41
Pettai 36
Kurichi 41
268

Chrisitian Historical Society, a Christian researchers fellowship which empower, engage, enrich christian history and preserve Christian contributions to indian society. Christian Historical Society itself run by volunteers, theologians and Historians. Last three years our society has done various projects like field research, digitization, multimedia podcasting, social media proclamation for the goodness of Indian christianity and the Kingdom of God. Especially for the empowerment of future christian generations, our society publishes a Christian History research periodical called "Christhava Varalatru Suvadugal". For the Enrichment, and Engagement of christian knowledge Chrsitian Historical Society re-publishes the old christian books.